CROWN OF EMPIRE

OTHER BOOKS BY PAUL ELDRIDGE

CROWN
OF EMPIRE

THE STORY OF NEW YORK STATE

Paul Eldridge

New York · THOMAS YOSELOFF · *London*

To Sylvette
Companion Incomparable
of All My Crossroads

Contents

Illustrations

(The illustrations appear as a group following page 128)

9

Traffic along the Erie Canal, near Palatine Bridge
Route 9, with a view of Lake George

> (*All the photographs in this book have been reproduced by courtesy of NYSPIX, New York State Department of Commerce*)

CROWN OF EMPIRE

1 A Place in the Sun

IT is called the Empire State—but it is crowded in by Vermont, Massachusetts, Connecticut on the East, by New Jersey and Pennsylvania on the South, by Pennsylvania on the West, and, northward, pushed by all of these into the middle of the waters of Lakes Ontario and Erie where they are stopped by Canada.

The waters of the two nations mix fraternally and so do their people. Still, imagine such a state not in North America, but in Europe or in the Middle East. How insecure, how precarious its very existence. How often the boots of its neighbors—therefore its enemies—would have resounded through all the hundreds of Main Streets of its cities and towns, would have trampled its fields of wheat and buckwheat, rye and corn! Or had it itself been maddened by ambition—racial, religious—what havoc it would have caused all around. A word—coined by a maniac, dipped in the gall of hate—might have turned the rivers into blood and the highways into vast cemeteries.

Merely gazing at the map teaches a lesson in common sense, good will, and democracy. Here is a promise of the "One World" whose birth-pangs all mankind endures at this moment—the one world that will arrive when it becomes evident that the Earth is indivisible, that rivers but heal and bind the ruptured shores and mountains seal the planetary wounds.

Who was the merry wag who crowned the State (for it was not with ill or solemn intent, as empires are generally named)? New York would certainly raise a monument to his memory, but he made his grandiose gesture and vanished forever. The State is as proud of its title as a high degree Mason of his uniform. (This, too, is profoundly and uniquely American—this love for titles with no validity in law. Let a princeling or a duchess set foot on our soil, and the nation is all aflutter. But has any one in his senses ever proposed to Congress that the United States of America set up a system of titles, hereditary or otherwise, with all the rights and privileges appertaining thereto?)

Yet, in a generation of pasters of labels and hurlers of epithets, older nations, unaccustomed to our youthful pranks, might see in the word "Empire" a menace to peace and security, even as we might see in their innocent ancient appellations the advent of Anti-Christ and the day of doom.

So let us not imagine our State a flat mass on a flat map. Let us always remember that the Earth is round and in space, and that the State of New York is neighbor to faraway lands, to strange peoples with strange tongues and strange customs. We must remember this, or we shall not understand why the Empire State has such significance—and perhaps an even greater destiny.

The Empire State is a great state, and in a period when "big" and "great" are so often confounded we must emphasize that it is indeed great. It is big, too, if we compare it to the little nations of Europe—even to the bigger ones, like England, which it almost equals. But among her sister states, New York ranks the twenty-ninth.

Its greatest length from east to west is 326 miles (or 412 if you include Long Island). From north to south it measures 312 miles. Its total area is 49,204 square miles, of which 1550 square miles are water.

New York is the antique of American geology; a land of rocks older than legends. In the northern lobe of the state are rocks nowhere surpassed in hoariness. The high peak area of the Adirondack region is made up of a rock called anorthosite, similar in age and mixture to that which forms the foundation of the skyscrapers of New York City. Thus the fairy tale of the past made possible the fairy tale of the present, for the city of New York is as much a reality as an incredible tale.

The Adirondack Mountains constitute the state's most prominent features. They extend southward to the Valley of the Mohawk and westward to the slope which descends from Lake Champlain. Upon their colossal backs they carry vast forests of fir and ash and spruce and, above the timber line, hardy plants of the Alpine zone. The spruce and birch tower eighty feet in the air. Generations of fallen leaves serve as their carpet and their quilt and prove to the thoughtful mountaineer that the finality of death is an illusion and that, as life carries its seed of destruction, so death carries its root of resurrection.

Where the trees are less serried and the sun and the rain can penetrate sufficiently, you will find star flowers and trilliums and the enchanter's nightshade (ah, the witchery of words) and the Indian pipe and goldthread are not too scarce. And dandelions grow one foot tall, crowns of gold.

Out of man's inhumanity to trees vast populations of them have been cut and only niggardly replaced. Still, where the forests have been only lightly touched, the scenery is wild and grand.

The ancient inhabitants of the Adirondacks have vanished, but not without leaving their signatures in the shape of fossils—mammoth, mastodon, and the giant beaver of the Ice Age.

To the now-legendary beasts man has been as unkind as he is periodically in war against his own generations. He liquidated the bison with the Indians. The wild turkey followed, and the timber wolf and the otter, and the mink's new habitat is milady's back. The wolverine had already made his exit by 1811; the elk said adieu in 1840; the moose at the beginning of the Civil War.

The woodchuck still runs these mountains, and the porcupine, and the muskrat and the pine marten; the mole and the raccoon, the chipmunk and the red squirrel, the hare and the fox and the bear live and multiply. These are yet targets for the gunner, but let him beware. The day of the great and free slaughter is over. There is conservation legislation now, and when he least expects it, justice grabs him by the collar.

While we are visiting with our brothers, the animals, the ancient and the modern, we must not neglect our sisters, the birds (although man's visit seems nowhere particularly desirable). There are nearly three hundred species of the feathered ones, many magnificent in color and delightful in sound. Some are year-rounders, others only tourists of the summer months.

Let us call a partial roster of these creatures who most nearly resemble the angels. We shall start with the sparrow for, despite its nuisance value, it has the virtue of being the humblest of them all and counts upon our pity rather than upon our admiration and love. Then come the catbird, the bluebird, the woodpecker, the barn swallow, the meadow lark, the cuckoo, the hawk, the kingfisher, the grouse, the wood thrush—and who would ignore the robin?

St. Francis of Assisi concentrated his affection and his preaching upon beasts and birds, but he did not disdain the fish. Nor shall we. The New York waters have worlds of inhabitants. Lake Champlain has pike and smelt, whitefish and bass. The Upper Hudson is host to whitefish, trout, sculpin. The Raquette River of the northern Adirondacks breeds the typical cool-water species. Lake Erie has the white bass. The smaller streams have trout, bass, and suckers. The waters bathing Long Island have flounder and crab and starfish. The fisherman need not worry. He requires only rod, bait, time, and patience. Grandiose stories are sure to follow.

The first and irrevocable law of Nature is that there be no favorites in her domains—no master tree and no slave shrub, no master beast and no slave insect, no hierarchy of flesh and fin and feather. We dispute neither her wisdom nor her justice, and we shall not ignore our State's "pests." There is the mosquito (not, however, a malaria carrier), but there are, besides, great efforts in the direction of swamp drainage and much success. Without being unneighborly, we have but to point our finger to New Jersey. That's a mosquito state for you. How lustily they whizz there, how adroitly they stab. The Empire State is not a mosquito state, but the pests within her borders are various and legion.

Now that we have named the pests, we can add the useful insect life, the praying mantis—magnificent creature—the dragon fly, the lady beetle, the moth. The butterfly, the Don Juan of the wings, we shall mention by himself, and to the bee we shall grant a special niche. The bee and the cow, mothers of man. Milk and honey—without which, where is civilization? And, of course, the cricket and the ant—the genesis of all morality.

If you have something of the cricket in your heart you should certainly love the Adirondacks both in the summer and in the winter. Perhaps you are a climber. Try Mt. Marcy, the highest peak, only 5345 feet. A little more modest in your ways—you might attempt Mt. McIntyre, Mt. Haystack, Mt.

Skylight. But even if the prudence of the ant is in your blood, you would still enjoy the Adirondack State Park— 5,575,000 acres of private and public mountain—two-thirds of the great lobe of the State north of the Mohawk River between Lake Champlain and Lake Ontario. Like spiders' silver webs the rivers meander and glow, the lakes, the ponds glint. And there is one continuous chain of lakes in which you can canoe for 150 miles. And there are (if the arches of your feet will bear it) 500 miles of foot trails. And there is skiing.

For those who are interested—there are about two hundred campsites in the Adirondacks and the Catskills for the vacationing public, at little expense. The Conservation Department furnishes circulars and wisdom warns that one should abide by the regulations and avoid difficulties.

The rich require neither the information nor the admonition. They reside in the magnificent private estates which surround Lake George, south of Lake Champlain. It is considered, and with reason, one of the most beautiful mountain lakes in the world.

The Catskills are not as high as the Adirondacks and not so imposing. Nevertheless, you would not consider a summer ill spent in one of the multitudinous resorts situated upon their flanks or in the valleys. The Catskills form a group, rather than a range, to the south of the Mohawk Valley. The elevations range from two to four thousand feet. Slide Mountain, the highest, has an altitude of 4205. To the west of the mountains lies the narrow valley of the Hudson River which, in the lower part of its course, cuts its way through one of these ranges, forming the beautiful Highland Region.

Of the Hudson we shall have much more to say later on, but here we urge you as a patriotic duty to love the River and its Valley, even if you are impervious to natural beauty.

For here Fenimore Cooper peopled the forests with immortal heroes and Washington Irving carved deathless legends. Rip Van Winkle, for instance, and those mountain dwarfs who carried barrels on their backs. (Less than a couple of centuries later full-grown Americans were weighted with mere flasks upon their hips. What degeneration.) Cooper and Irving were our first ambassadors to Europe who were not laughed out of court. For a nation that has no literature has no official standing. It may even be said that its very existence is precarious.

West of the Catskills, occupying all of the southern and central parts of the State and extending to its western boundary, is the great plateau region. Rivers have cut deep valleys here and there are a number of depressions formed by glacial action, many of which are occupied by lakes. The terrace farthest inland is formed by a crest of limestone—the escarpment over which Niagara Falls plunges.

Niagara Falls, the dinosaur of the waters. Who shall describe the glow, the roar, the might of the giant in a world dedicated to pygmyism of the spirit? What dithyrambic bard shall we awaken from his ancient tomb; what Goliath to thunder the lines?

No, it is best that you go and see for yourself. Stand in wonderment as the millions who preceded you stood in wonderment. And if you happen to be on your honeymoon, so much the better. Every couple, regardless of age, is suspected there. You are sure to be in style.

But we shall give you some of the physical details. The Falls are both on the American and the Canadian sides. On the American side the water is of less depth—1060 feet—and of comparatively small volume; the Canadian Falls are 1230 feet across and of much greater volume. The Falls discharge at the rate of 500,000 tons a minute. The land on each side of the Falls has been converted into parks. The State of New York reserves and controls 107 acres, the Dominion government 154 acres.

And once again we see how fortunate we were—and how intelligent—that we did not construct fortresses and did not plant spies and sentinels, for surely then the parks would have been battle-fields and the foamy waters of the Falls would forever have been stained with the blood of men.

We have set our State in space. We have made a rapid sketch of its physiognomy. We have put in some mountains, rivers, lakes, some fauna and flora. We shall return in good time to fill the lacunae, to smooth the picture. But for a while now, we shall make the acquaintance of those who gave it its birth and its significance, for in the final count nothing has meaning except in terms of man. All things point to man, and the sun and the moon and the earth exist because man exists, man and his imagination.

2 Immigrants All

WHEN a Puritan Father wrote the chronicle of his town, he started with the creation of the world, Adam and Eve, the original sin, the multitudinous events in which his brave ancestors took major roles, and their inevitable voyage to the New World, finally to settle and found, say, Bailey (no longer on the map), population 936 (all gamboling in the clover fields of Paradise).

The Puritan Father did not err. All events are links in a chain. They cannot be foretold but they can be retold. The Puritan Father did not err, but he sinned, for he spoke out of vanity, not out of truth.

The State of New York was destined from all eternity to become a mighty state, to be peopled with men of energy, to grow wealthy and famous. The man who named it "The Empire State" spoke with the clairvoyance of a prophet. The State of New York is a natural empire. Its geographical position, its physical features, its waterways, its valleys, its resources are magnets that inevitably pull man and stir his energies and his ambitions.

No other area on the North American Continent offers such variety in landscape; no soil is so hospitable to numerous types of vegetation. The alluvial plains are covered by soil which rewards its tiller with vegetables and grain far beyond his efforts. And the climate has those variations that stimulate the blood and the brain of man.

21

The State of New York had but to bide its time and it was certain to be crowned. And what mattered a few more millennia? Only man is in a hurry. Only man has no time. Only man has visions of centuries—and paltry days in which to follow them.

When did man first settle in the New York region? All indications point to a relatively recent date. Certainly neither the rock shelters nor the caves offer us evidence that man inhabited this region during the glacial or immediate postglacial periods. The glacial till and the ancient gravel present us with neither tools nor other objects undeniably made by human hands. There are no artifacts, and the rude flints discovered are not indicative of great age.

Man has been upon Earth for perhaps a half-million years, but upon this continent, and certainly in the State of New York, he seems to have been only within historic times. The day may come when archeologists (whom we bury in forgetfulness, but who deserve our profoundest gratitude for mental liberation) will find some hidden treasures to make us completely change our opinion; all knowledge must remain tentative. Tentativeness indeed, is the glory of science, while peddlers of ignorance advertise their unalterable prejudices.

Hunger or fear or adventure or boredom drove certain Asiatic tribes across the Bering Straits into the North Land. Despite all hardships, despite quarrels and efforts at mutual extermination, they not only survived but multiplied, and spread southward along the western coast, then eastward across mountains and deserts, through wild forests and over wilder rivers.

There were, probably, several millions of these both in North and South America, before any considerable number began crossing the Rocky Mountains and settling along the Atlantic Coast.

These early immigrants left us nothing to remember them by. Nomads, they wandered from one spot to another settling where food seemed more accessible or danger less likely. Along the Hudson headwaters some old sites were discovered, but how old they are archeologists will not venture to guess. Certainly, they cannot say that they are the oldest, or try to identify the tribe that first used the tools discovered there, for tribe followed tribe, either by conquest or by emigration, and it is safer, for the time being at least, to let things hang in the air.

But who are these Asiatic people who invaded the New World when it was ancient? The ten lost tribes of Israel, some pseudo-historians claim. The truth is that we do not know who these immigrants were, except that they antedated the Daughters of the American Revolution by many centuries, and that they too were refugees.

Despite the wide distribution of the aboriginal dwellers of these parts, we observe fairly uniform physical characteristics, and we must come to the conclusion that they were one race. As it always happens, however, the habitat of a people will in time shape it and finally differentiate it from its original trunk. The immigrants to this continent gradually became "Americans" and only vaguely resembled their ancestral Asiatics, save, perhaps, in the pigmentation of their skin, a red-brown hue. Nor is there any similarity between the languages of the Americans and the languages of Asia.

When the tribes reached the State, they already had a high degree of civilization—organized warfare, face painting, belief in supernatural beings, prayers for rain and fertility, sacrifices in the form of burnt tobacco so that the nostrils of the gods in the "land of the sky" might be delighted and give them in return strength and cunning to defeat the enemy and scalp him and steal his property.

The tribes settled along the shores of the Hudson, painting and engraving rocks and trees with insignia to show proprietary rights of hunting and fishing in certain areas.

The Lenape tribes occupied the western banks; the Raritans chose the mouth of the river; the Hackensacks, the Tappans, and the Haverstraws considered the wooded north their own. These formed the confederation of Unami, the Turtle. Another Lenape confederation was the Minsi, the Wolf, whose chief tribes were the Waranawankongs, the Catskills, and the Wawarsings.

Across the Hudson from the Lenape were the Manhattans and the Wappingers. Near what are now Lake George and Lake Champlain was the home of the strongest of the Algonquins, the Mohicans, "people-of-the-water-that-flows-two-ways," as they called the Hudson.

The tribes along the Hudson built their huts in imitation of the hills—wooden bowls, bottoms up. A hole in the center of the roof served for the escape of the smoke of the fireplace built deep in the ground. On long horizontal poles hung drying corn, food baskets, clothes. Curving benches around the inside walls were both chairs and beds.

The Iroquoian stock included the Cherokee, the Wyandot, the Huron, the confederated Five Nations, the Erie, the Neutral, the Tuscarora. They held a great portion of New York and often were in dispute with the Algonquins over their territory. Neither the linguistic stocks nor the territorial areas ever became fixed, however, and no Balkans ever witnessed more numerous disputes and more frequent changes of boundaries.

Patrols watched over landmarks, and woe to the outer tribesman who dared to trespass the hunting grounds. The areas were sometimes agreed upon, however, in council, and observed for a time. But hunger, adventure, ambition, make of any treaty a scrap of paper, and the attitudes of Niccolo Machiavelli are not limited to Florentines.

During the periods of peace (created chiefly by isolation and by abundance of food) the tribes developed their various cultures. They never reached any very specialized type, however, for there was not time enough between skirmishes. These were not always the result of human malignity. Nature, too, added her share in the form of droughts and storms, or wild beasts which roamed in vast numbers, destroying vegetation and making life precarious.

Nevertheless, there *were* peace-loving tribes with a sense of prudence. They stored food and utensils, but they were subject to raids by their less thrifty brethren. Therefore, they learned to build fortifications and stockades. These protected them but also proved their undoing, for defense, as we have learned in our generation, never wins wars, and Maginot Lines destroy the will to fight.

Among these pacific tribes, the River Indians—known as the Mannahatta or the Shatemuc—who inhabited the shores of the Hudson, were particularly pleasant. They were a kindly folk, handsome and tall. The whites, when they appeared upon the American scene, found only one fault with them—their smell did not please their nostrils. In the long and terrible history of racial hatred, we often come across the nasal discomfort the stronger experiences at contact with the weaker. What the weaker felt is rarely recorded, for history is largely the glorification of the iniquities of the triumphant. However, in this particular instance, there seems to be a justifiable cause. The River Indians had the custom of rubbing with the greases of slain beasts their upper bodies, which were exposed to the sun (prototypes of the present generation of Americans at the shore resorts, save for the grace of perfume).

The lower half of the Indian's body was encased in a breech clout, leggings of tanned hide, hip-length and soft-soled moccasins. Unlike their Western relatives, they did not wear the long feather war bonnets (later adapted in more or less modified forms by the white ladies of high degree on the warpath of amour, except that the feathers of the Indians were not aigrets requiring the murder of countless nests of fledglings). The Indians, instead, burned off with hot stones most of their hair, leaving one lock running from the fore-head to the nape of the neck—the scalp lock so highly prized by their enemies.

The squaws wore shorter than knee-length leather aprons about their waists, moccasins, and beaded caps which cov-ered the long braids of their raven hair. In the winter both men and women sported robes of wolf, bear, or deer skins and mantles of turkey feathers, glittering magnificently as the winds ruffled the edges.

The aesthetic sense of our foster forebears was not much below our own. They painted their faces and bodies with dyes made from the juices of berries; their necks tinkled and glowed with shells of all the colors of their Mother, the Sea; on their chests hung pendants of stones of numberless shapes. And the squaws, true daughters of Eve, covered their clothes with shell beads, as symbol of affluence and social standing.

The shores of the Hudson were not extensively devoted to agriculture, since in many places they were too steep and the rock was too near the surface. Yet, in their clearings, the women raised maize, beans, and pumpkins, while their lords and masters fished and hunted or, sitting on their haunches, plunged in deep contemplation of nothing.

Life was comparatively easy for the Indian in the country destined to become the Empire State. The land was a good mother, affording him abundant food even when he neglected to sow. There were plenty of "greens" to be plucked, berries to be gathered, barks pleasant to the palate, not to mention the honeyed sap of birch and maple.

Meat there was aplenty. The forests teemed with animal life. Pigeons "flew like clouds and darkened the sun, and when they alighted they broke down the branches of trees beneath their weight." Then there were wild ducks and wild turkeys and geese and grouse and squirrels, and the hills swarmed with deer and bear and raccoon. And no matter how strong the wing, how fast the leg, how sharp the eye, the arrow was faster and stronger and the snare had more cunning.

The big game not only filled the belly but covered the body. What vestments more appropriate for a denizen of the forest, both for warmth and durability, than the skin of the elk; what quilt warmer than the skin of the bison?

The forest had more riches still. The bark of trees supplied him with material for houses and canoes, with ropes and cords, and the learned ones culled the herbs for medicinal purposes.

As for the River, it was a veritable father, rich beyond all computation. Practically for the asking you could get sturgeon and shad and striped bass and herring and eel, and in the shallows you could pick enough oysters to replete yourself with vitamins and the lust of life.

The region of the present State of New York was inhabited chiefly by the Algonquian tribes, followed later by the more bellicose Iroquoian tribes. The Algonquians came in waves over long periods of time. The earliest period has yielded to the archeologist crude implements, clumsy spears, clay pottery, and occasionally a polished stone implement. It is evidently a period influenced by the Eskimo.

The later occupation is characterized by flints, steatite pottery, grooved axes, hoes, copper implements, clay pipes, roller pestles, bone implements, awls, harpoons, needles, and beads. Graves are already found, the skeletons doubled up on one side, but no artifacts accompany the dead. Let the dead bury the dead.

On certain Algonquian sites, effigies of human faces or heads have been discovered, and they seem to be well modeled. They are either of wood or stone, while the stone pipes are frequently beautifully carved, some having animals in relief.

The Iroquois were more ingenious in their tools, weapons, and utensils, and their artistic efforts show remarkable talent. In the historic period they already had towns on the lowlands near the shores of Lake Erie and Ontario. Their mortuary customs were rather different from those of the Algonquians. They had, indeed, several customs, probably indicating several periods of their migration. Sometimes the human remains are found beneath the ground, buried intact. At other times the body was wrapped in blankets or skins and placed in the branches of large trees. There were also ossuaries of fifty to a hundred remains. In the individual graves the body is fixed in a sleeping position, knees toward the head, hands toward the face, sometimes accompanied by burial objects— pipes, knives, pots, shell objects—everything to make the deceased comfortable and give him a start in his new life.

The Iroquois house was made of bark and several families dwelt together. The consanguinity was matriarchal. The women nominated the sachems and could veto the decisions of the tribal council. Whether there ever was a rebellion against "momism" such as is raging in our country today is nowhere recorded.

Chivalry can hardly go beyond making woman the creator of the world and all the good things therein, but the Iroquois cosmogony points in that direction. Cleared of many irrelevancies, it seems that in the beginning of the world a pregnant woman fell from heaven upon the back of a turtle and gave birth to a female child, who in turn gave birth to two sons, the Light One and the Dark One. The Dark One, insisting upon emerging through her armpit, killed the mother. The grandmother took care of the two boys, and bade them watch their mother's grave. From her grave sprang all the food plants and tobacco; from her eyes the sun and the moon. The Dark or Evil One continued to prosper, and that is not legend but truth.

The Algonquians, whom we shall meet later on as the first to encounter and do business with the white man (if bartering islands for beads and bartering souls for aqua vitae may be called business), were a happy folk and industrious. Male and female did their chores. A false rumor has been circulating for too long that the Indian woman did all the work and the Indian man had but to grumble his wishes.

The white man need not sigh for those "golden days," for the Indian, like himself, did his share fully. He fished, hunted, fought, cleared the land, built the stockades, cut the trees, built the houses, which in his gallantry he bequeathed to his wife. The Indian woman, on her part, planted the land, cooked, dressed the hides, and was the mother.

There was pleasure for all. There were games and dances and songs. There was swimming and rowing and wrestling. And there was love—of all joys the deepest and of all pains the sharpest, but even the pain of love was sweet. And love brought papooses into the world, and was any bird's song as merry as their voices and was the laughter of the Neebanawbaigs, the happy water spirits, half as delicious?

And at night, after the family had eaten the roasted meats and the maize bread, weather permitting, they would sit outside of their houses and smoke and watch the new moon which Minewawa, goddess of the valley, had just hung above the peaks, for the old one she had cut into little stars and scattered all over the "land of the sky." They knew the dancing of the constellations quite well and could reckon by their changing positions when to plant and when to harvest. The stars were faithful and always predictable. Minewawa, however, being female, was capricious. You could never tell when you displeased her and provoked her to hurl sheaves of lightning at you and growl worse than a hundred packs of wolves in the dead of night. But, of course, she was a darling, too. Didn't she send the rain which lifted the maize out of the mud and puffed the golden cheeks of the pumpkin?

There was also the Sun, the Big Father, but who dared look him in the face? As for the spirits, they butted into everything, everywhere, always looking for trouble unless properly appeased. And did not the Wahwahtaysee, the fireflies, try so hard to show man where the black monsters were hiding in the rushes? Too bad that their lanterns went out always as you were about to catch sight of the Pukwidjinny, the dwarf.

Were there bright little doubters pestering their elders with unanswerable questions about spirits and the like, as they do among us? And did they survive their questions? Or did Manitou, chief of all spirits, enraged, come to tear the rebel spirit out of the rebel mouth—with the help, naturally, of the witch doctor's knife? What cyclone is comparable to the fury of superstition? What sceptered power has not thundered: "Incredible—therefore, believe!"

The sachem, the chief, devoted himself to the welfare of the people by means of peaceful pursuits. He was as a great tree for all the tribe to rest under, rejoice, and multiply.

When war broke out, however, he transferred his power to the "Hero," the general.

And wars broke out. For there are always the bad neighbors who prefer arrows to agriculture, the bad neighbors who envy and plunder and murder and glory in the desolation they bring upon others.

The bad neighbors wear heavy boots which reverberate through street and valley or they pad their moccasins so that their steps are lighter than the paws of prowling wolves —but all swoop upon their victims, who are never prepared, are never united, who say, "As long as it is not us, why bother helping our brothers?"

And so it happened that when the Iroquois—Mohawks, Cayugas, Onondagas, Oneidas, Senecas—made their terrifying appearances, the Algonquians had to submit. The tribute they had to pay was so high that, despite the riches of the River, the fecundity of the beasts of the hills and their own industry, they had to live in poverty and misery. Worse still, many of them were taken away, forced to abjure their tribes and join the conquerors.

But evil days beyond their imagination were to befall them when the "superior race" of pale-faced men would lose their way as they sought a shorter route to India and her riches and set foot on their land.

We shall take leave of them until that day arrives and return meanwhile to the physiognomy of our Empire State. Now that we have made it alive with man, we shall further see why man came here and why he remained here and why he prospered.

3 Hudson— River of Destiny

A N organism is alive when there is adequate circulation within and proper communication without. Every living being is constructed for these two processes. This is the rhythm eternal.

However rich in flora and fauna our State might be, however beautiful to gaze upon, it would have been dead for the history of man, if Nature had not also added the gift of circulation and communication.

Is Nature teleological? Is each stitch of her vast pattern loomed upon a previously-drawn design? Is man bound forever to the chariot of the merciless Kings, Cause and Effect? Is he like a stone which, hurled into the air, must return willy nilly to the Earth? Is he the proud weaver of his own destiny?

Be that as it may, whether fortuitous concourse of circumstances or deliberate planning, the Empire State definitely had the essential ingredients of circulation and communication.

But first came the legs. We who grow fat and dyspeptic in our automobiles have the impression that gas and tires mean locomotion. But without legs all movement ceases. The poets, wisest of men, knew this, and *their* invention was not something on wheels but boots—seven-league boots for the *legs*.

And before the legs of men came the legs of the beasts.

In their seasonal migrations, the big game animals tracked deeply into the earth and made paths through the wilderness of primeval forests. Their instinct led them to the lands which provided them with food, salt, and water. The Indian wanted both the animals and the lands. He had but to follow in their tracks, and thus unconsciously carved a life-giving circulation for himself.

But all this zigzaging across mountain and valley might, at most, have made of the State of New York a suitable habitat for primitive peoples—makers of legends, not of history. A land-locked nation sooner or later is choked. "Water! Water!" is the cry of living, growing things.

And how generous have been the gods of water to the Empire State. How manifold their gifts—lakes, streams, rivers, and an ocean. The Great Lakes to the north not only are largely responsible for the fertility of the plains, but made possible the transportation of heavy loads, while the Indian canoe found the vast system of streams and tributaries navigable to the very headwaters. North, south, east, west, the liquid paths united man to man for trade, barter, exchange of culture and of knowledge—and, alas, for war. And later on, forts were erected at all portages and suitable landing places, and from these towns and cities were born and thrived. Evil is ever close to good.

All these waters would have made New York prosperous, to be sure, and strong, but not the monarch of the states. One great river, like a mighty artery, pumped wealth and glory and fame into its body, the River-That-Flows-Both-Ways, the River of Destiny, the Hudson.

No cat—not even Pasht, the pussy moon goddess worshiped by the Egyptians before the Golden Calf usurped the Throne of the Universe—had as many lives as the Hudson. Nor will there be found in any Hall of Records a multi-

married heiress with as many names. Nor has there ever
blossomed a stately oak or strutted a self-made man whose
beginnings were humbler or more inauspicious—"a minute,
unpretending tear of the clouds."

Once upon a time a cool, shallow sea spread over the face
of what we now call New York. The rocks, tombstones to
the centuries, have it writ within them in the sacred tongue
of truth, which deprives all the little legends of creation of
their luster and their humor.

The sea spread northward into Canada and southward beyond Alabama. There were shores, but the rivers carried the
clay and the fine sand as tribute to the sea, and made beds—
tier upon tier—for myriad generations of animals to pro-
create and die upon, for the bed is the beginning and the
end of all.

These animals were one-celled, and the plants were no
bigger but already they showed their true colors. The plants
lived innocently on water and salts and sunlight, while the
animals devoured not only the plants but one another, and
still do. And millions of years later, when the lamb complained bitterly against the wolf and asked for justice, Gane-
sha, God of Wisdom, smiled, his eyes closing slowly: "What
small teeth you have, oh melancholy lamb!"

But the devourer and the devoured, alike no favorites of
Fate, ended by becoming beds of marble which added to the
beds of clay and of sand turned into vast masses thousands
of feet thick. Like a bully, a block of land floated from the
east and pushed into them and hardened them into shale
and limestone, squeezing the sea-water out of them, and the
State of New York was created. But no one saw that "it was
good," and there was only the roar of the mountains rising,
shaking all things.

The hot waters from under the crust like measureless lizards crawled upward and the folds of the beds grew hot and once again they changed their nature. Now they became mica-crystals and graphite. They are still with us in New York City and along the Palisades. No cauldron ever seethed as did the rocks and the mica and the quartz in the hot juices within the bowels of the Earth. And no witches ever stirred such fantastic destinies.

Masses of molten rocks burst into schists covering hundreds of square miles north in the Adirondacks and south along the shores of the present-day Hudson. Out in the open, the rocks cooled off with the same unhurried tempo with which they had previously melted. Millions of years passed, and there were high mountains extending all the way down to Alabama. These are known as the Older Appalachians. They were the roots of the newer Appalachians formed by the later accumulation of rocks. But these, too, were leveled by the waters that crossed them and carried their precious body into the Atlantic, as well as by the rains and the frost and the air which plague all mountains as if envious of their grandeur.

At last the mountains succumbed, and the State of New York, except for the present Catskills and the Adirondacks, was level again.

Meanwhile, the one-celled beings, plants and animals, distinguishable from one another chiefly by the murderous propensities of the latter, had changed. There were many varieties of plants and seaweeds now, ancestors of all our botanical life, and there were jellyfishes and sponges and snails and worms. And after a little while—a few more million years—there came the lobsters and the crabs and that pearly-chambered nautilus which was destined to become a fable of high courage and moral purpose for the school children of America.

And still no Hudson River. There were many rivers, but they were all nameless workers digging and forming the bed for the "Grande Rivière," one of the Hudson's appellations.

After millions of years of stress and strain the ancient rocks of the Older Appalachians finally cracked and split open. Released, rocks on the northwest rose, forming a range including the Hudson Highlands, the Ramapo and Schooley Mountains. The other shoulder, on the southeast, sank, forming a basin in northern New Jersey and southwestern New York. Rivers tumbled down the range into the basin, carrying along pebbles, sand, and clay, brown and rusty red because of the iron oxides. And the monarch of all he surveyed now was His Majesty the Dinosaur. How proudly he walked on his hind legs, seventy feet of rattling scales and bony plates balancing a tiny head, restless in its vanity. A thorough conservative, he. What was good for his ancestors was good enough for him. Let the world change—he would not. And the world changed—and he *was* not.

In the lava of the volcanoes that were active in the New Jersey area, the dinosaur left his footprints and his strides, which now grace New York City's American Museum of Natural History at 70th Street and Amsterdam Avenue. What actress pressing her dainty feet into the asphalt of Hollywood will be so honored a million years hence? (What being will study the fossil of an animal who, in his vanity, called himself *homo sapiens* but who in truth was *homo stultus,* for the first law of intelligence is the ability to adapt oneself to a changed environment.)

Still no Hudson. This is the Cretaceous Period—the period of "chalk" when chalk was still alive. Now there were giant sharks and saw-toothed reptiles and fishes which murdered one another and devoured one another. Man was already foreshadowed.

There were many birds, too. Did they sing? Were there ears to hear? Were there hearts to thrill? Were there barbed things to pierce their breasts that the songs be ripe with the honey of pain?

The salt sea rolled over the Atlantic States and most of the land was hidden by the waters, while the little rivers kept on washing gravel and sand and clay.

The Adirondack Mountains resisted. Battered and torn, they still remained the hills north of the seashore and made a cradle for the new river—"A minute, unpretending tear of the clouds—a lovely pool shivering in the breeze of the mountains." That's what it was when the famous naturalist Verplanck Colvin saw it and was overcome with emotion. Lake Tear of the Clouds, officially named, was already a million years old. Peak Marcy—the Tahawus, the Cloud Splitter—mirrors itself in the "Tear." East of it, the dome, Haystack; to the north, Table Top; to the south, Skylight; to the west, Mount McIntyre.

Clear and cool, the "tear" spills over its rocks, as over cheeks, to Feldspar Brook, and through its ripples glitter the stones—its bed of green and gold and blue—the iridescent labradorite.

As it flows down it meets other brooks—the Up Hill and the Upper Twin. From Flowed Lands and the Falls of Hanging Spear descending through the shadow of Calamity Mountain another fork joins it, and all together form the Opalescent River which, running south and then west, becomes the Hudson at the hill town of Newcomb.

A little uncertain of itself, it flows south to Indian River Junction and between Bad Luck and Kettle Mountains, then east of the steep sides of Ruby and Balm of Gilead until it merges with the noisy Schroon. With all these waters in its arteries, it dashes south, strong and wide, between friendly

shores broken by three mouths of streams—Stony Creek, Wolf
Creek, the Sacandaga River. Now it drops into an old north–
south channel which deepens as it runs, and finally flows
through a gorge within an older valley.

The floor of the gorge lies below the level of the sea,
creating a fiord into which the ocean tides invade the fresh
waters. Now the Hudson runs south through a land of ice-
built terraces to the northern gate of its highland canyon.
On the west there are the folded floors of ancient tropic seas,
while on the east lie the Taconics, older than the Catskills.

The River pursues its way past the peaks Storm King and
Breakneck, past Mount Taurus on the east, Bear Mountain
on the west, between Dundenberg and Anthony's Nose, past
High Tor and Prickly Pear Hill. It widens to more than three
and a half miles as it reaches Haverstraw Bay. Beyond this
point it begins to narrow, and the west side becomes a col-
umned wall 550 feet in height—the Palisades, which the Indians called Wehawken, "Rocks-that-resemble-trees."

And now the River runs past the narrow island which in
the early documents of its history was spelled in forty-one
ways—Manhattes, Manhates, Manhatton, Manhattans, Manhattan—into New York Bay, and thence between Staten Island on the west and Long Island on the east, until it finally
finds its terminus in the Atlantic.

But the end of its channel is not yet. It cuts into the bed
of the ocean which millions of years ago dropped fifteen
thousand feet, seven times deeper than the Royal Gorge of
Colorado. Alas, that poets were not upon the Earth to sing
the marvels of those giant days! Now in the pygmy days
there *are* poets, but none to listen to them.

A mighty river gushed out of the ice sheets that covered
the Hudson Valley and roared downward for thousands of
years, but the time came when the salt sea returned, swal-

lowed the river, and buried the canyon. Over it, now, waves undulate like fields of grasses covering the graves of those who in life had dreams higher than mountains and despairs deeper than gorges.

Three miles southeast of Ambrose Lightship the Hudson Submarine Channel begins and runs in a sweeping curve, broadening and deepening until, ninety miles from its inception, it is covered by its delta, forming Glens Falls, Hudson Falls and Baker's Falls. Three miles southeast of this delta was the original mouth of the abyss, five and a half miles across from lip to lip.

In the Hudson gorge beings dwell beyond the conjuration of fevered minds. There is the blind fish, for instance, whose eye-pockets are headlights luring compatriots to their doom. There is a tiny fish like a white thread whose eyes stick far out on spindle legs. There is that silver round fish like a chain about a prosperous stomach. His eyes are always raised heavenward, praying while preying—the spawn of Bigot and Mammon. There are the violet hunchbacked shrimp and the shrimp exuding clouds of scarlet flames. There is the black dragon, each fang a scimitar.

And so, for ages, new Hudsons were born and were swallowed up. Five times the glaciers formed and melted and sailed away. New hills, new valleys, new streams. Mammoth elephants shook the earth beneath their bulk and passed on to their reward; giant sloths dragged on and on, to become within a few thousand years a symbol of degradation and warning. The little horses with three toes that galloped across from Jersey to New York also vanished, and none of their descendants were seen in this part of the world until the Spaniards brought their proud cavalry to trample under hoof their frightened enemies.

But finally there was stability for a little while; ten thou-

sand years, a hundred thousand years? And man made his
appearance and the present Hudson River stayed in its
course. And now the waters—destined to be named the
Grande Rivière, the River of the Steep Hills, the San Antonio, the Río de Gomez, the Río de Guamas, the Norum-
bega, the Prince Mauritius, the Groote River, Manhattan
River, Nassau River, Noordt River, Montaigne River—flows
on between its beautiful shores, past great mountains, swal-
lowing many tributaries—Saw Mill River, Pocantico River,
Croton River, Peekskill Creek, Fishkill Creek, Wappinger
Creek, Fall Kill Creek, Casper Creek, Crum Flow Creek,
Landsman Kill, Stony Creek, Roeliff Jansen Kill, Kinderhook
or Stockport Kill, Moordener Creek, and Wynats Kill on the
east; and on the west, Popolopen Creek, Moodna Creek,
Quassaic Creek, Ronout River, Esopus Creek, Hans Vosen
Kill, Corlear Kill, Murderers Creek, Coeymans Creek, Baker
Creek, Vloman Kill, and Norman Kill.

All in all, from source to sea, the Hudson has a length of
three hundred miles—the first half of which bubbles and
rushes tempestuously, foaming over rocky barriers, plung-
ing over waterfalls, snatching tributaries. Reaching Troy and
Albany, however, the river turns sedate and moves on with
majestic tread to its terminus.

Has it become old in the interval? More than that. It has
become metamorphosed into a sea or semi-sea. At the beginning of its career it pours down from a great height, but
by the time it reaches midriff it is only six feet above sea level
and is met and stayed by insweeping tides. The Indians, with
their keen sight and an innate feeling for appropriate appellations, used to refer to it as "the-stream-that-flows-both-
ways."

The waters from the mountains lose their virgin sweetness,
become first brackish and then salt. But what they relinquish

in innocence they make up in strength, for henceforth the
Hudson is capable of carrying ocean-going vessels. A deep
fiord, it wends its way sometimes past precipices, sometimes
between hills, sometimes in the very shadows of mountains.
Indeed, if this intermarriage of waters had not occurred,
New York would have been an inland town gasping for
greatness.

Due north and south, in a straight line as one sails upon
the Hudson, one should be able to behold the towers of Albany and Troy, but a little bend in the course closes the
river into many charming cradles of water, each one seen
separately until one climbs the mountains, when they appear
as a string of pearls of some mute siren whose throat is still
smooth but who no longer has the will to entice. Or perhaps
there are no longer mariners worthy of conquest. To recall
the thunderous Odysseus and then to see the new slick captain, slave of a wheel and a lever!

But the time has come to leave the River to flow on and the
Redskins on its shores and its environs to pursue the rhythm
of their lives. We must wander a while in another world and
watch the loom upon which the pattern of the things to come
is woven. For there is no beginning and no end and all
things are circular.

4 The Loom

APRIL 17, 1492, and one Cristobal Colón or Cristoforo Colombo, later to be known as Christopher Columbus, signed the "Capitulations" or articles of contract with the government of Their Most Christian Majesties, Ferdinand and Isabella, recent deliverers of Spain from the rule of the Moors.

The articles conferred upon Columbus the title of Don and Admiral and the powers of viceroy and governor "in all the islands and lands which should be discovered and acquired" by him, the tenth part of "all the pearls, precious stones, gold, silver, spices and other merchandise" there found, as well as the right to subscribe one-eighth of the cost of the expedition and to have one-eighth of the profits.

Great honors and vast possibilities for a man who knocked at the doors for years vainly trying for an audience, rejected by his own compatriots, tricked by the scholars of Portugal, and for seven years imploring the same monarchs to hearken to his proposals.

Why was Isabella ready now to invest a colossal sum? Had she not depleted the coffers of state in the long war waged against the infidel, during whose regime there was neither Inquisition, nor expulsion, nor religious tyranny? She still had her jewels, and the romantic chroniclers speak of the gracious gesture of removing them from throat and finger and casket and offering them to the newly-created Admiral.

It is neither in the nature of woman nor certainly in the nature of queens to relinquish their precious possessions, particularly for a venture which had all the earmarks of madness.

But in the same month of the same year, a few days previous to the signing of the "Capitulations," a wonderful thing happened to Christian Spain. "After the Spanish monarchs had expelled all the Jews from all their Kingdoms and lands in April, in the same month they commissioned me to undertake the voyage to India," so writes Columbus.

What a windfall there was! "Pearls, precious stones, gold, silver and other merchandise" tumbled into the lap of Her Majesty! What a wonderful idea to get rid of the Jew! What a marvelous man Torquemada! Now Spain shall become the mightiest country in the world, the richest, the most beloved of the Lord! How fortunate for ancestors that they are not present when the descendants reap what they had sowed. It was not the flush of health that spread across the face of the Peninsula but the fever of injustice, which would in time consume her, until she would become the weakest, the poorest, the least blessed of the nations of the Earth. Her great cities became vast cemeteries; her people beggars on the streets; wars and revolutions never ceased. Injustice is a gibbet from which the judges sooner or later swing.

But in April 1492, Her Most Christian Majesty was so happy that she was willing to listen even to the most fantastic ideas of this sailor who insisted upon becoming Viceroy and Life-Governor of all the lands he might discover. His Most Christian Majesty, Ferdinand, was obdurate, but what can you expect of a man? Besides, Luis de Santangel knew the power of flattery, or else how had he escaped the stake when the rest of his family was purified by fire?

Luis de Santangel, the Marrano, knew, besides, that flat-

tery is most acceptable when backed by cash, and so he proposed to the Queen that he would show his confidence in the
Admiral by himself lending the government the sum of five
million maravedis, sufficient to finance the project.

What had Isabella to lose? Everybody knew what a Marrano's "lending" meant. If the enterprise proved successful,
why then all stood to win; if it failed, the former Jew alone
would be the loser. If ever he dared put in a claim against
the government, he would quickly be found guilty of wor-
shiping in the manner of his forefathers, tortured, burnt, and
the rest of his wealth confiscated. A marvelous system that
never failed. Except, of course, in the long run, but is a
Queen supposed to be clairvoyant? *Après moi le déluge,*
was spoken in many a tongue, in many a generation, before
Louis XV gave it final form.

The Queen graciously accepted, and Columbus began
getting ready. But money was not the only thing Columbus
received from Jews and Marranos. He received directly and
indirectly much of his knowledge of navigation, his astron-
omy, his mathematics. Jafuda Cresques, also known as Jaime
of Mallorca, the "Map Jew," director of the school of navigation at Sagres, had prepared a map of the world for King
Juan of Aragon and manufactured the finest nautical instruments of his day. Abraham Ben Samuel Zacuto, famous
astronomer and mathematician, encouraged Columbus per-
sonally, besides giving him his almanacs and astronomical
tables. Not to mention Don Isaac Abravanel and Abraham
Senior, two of the most prominent Jews in all of Spain, who
had confidence in Columbus and helped him financially and
morally.

But Columbus himself, who was he? A Genoese, perhaps
—born in 1446, perhaps. Who was his father, his mother?
Columbus was anything but inarticulate. He liked to talk, to

write. We have his journals. He speaks of many things in them but never of his antecedents. Why? Was he hiding anything? What? There was one thing people feared most in those days—to get into trouble with the Church. The wealthy in particular. But a poor sailor had nothing to fear—unless his history as a Christian was short, unless it became known that his father, for instance, had been the first in his family tree to abjure the faith of his ancestors, and in particular the Mosaic. For then he might be a Christian in public only, but in private he might still worship according to the ancient traditions of the Hebrews, be a Marrano—a hog. Was it this that bothered Columbus? Was it for this that he received so much encouragement from Jew and Neo-Christian? Did blood tell? Were there secret signs among them?

At any rate, Columbus chose among his sailors several Jews—Luis de Torres, baptized shortly before sailing, who knew Hebrew, Chaldaic and Arabic, and who would serve as an interpreter; Alfonso de Calle, Rodrigo Sanchez, Maestro Bernal, physician; Marco, surgeon—and others whose names have been lost.

The Decree of Expulsion of the Jews was proclaimed in April, but by another coincidence, as strange as the signing of the "Capitulations," the actual expulsion began on the second day of August, while Columbus set sail from Palos on the third day in his little fleet composed of the *Santa Maria* (230 tons), the *Pinta,* and the *Niña* (both somewhat smaller).

The boats carrying many of the expatriated and desperate Jews, most of them to death, sighted the fleet which was destined to open a new world for their descendants—a world in which they would have the privileges of freemen, even as their ancestors had had in Spain for eight centuries, during the reign of the "Infidel."

The trials and tribulations of the Admiral and his crew are schoolboy knowledge, and the date of his landing, October 12, 1492, is his holiday. Luis de Torres was sent ashore to parley with the inhabitants and thus became the first white man to step upon the soil of the new continent. It was not India, however, and his linguistic abilities served him but little, but he was so impressed with the copper-colored people, that he finally settled in Cuba for the remainder of his life and was the first one to introduce tobacco into the Old World. In describing, in a Hebrew letter to a Marrano in Spain, the strange things and animals of his new abode, Luis de Torres mentioned a bird, which he called "tukki" (it appears in I Kings, 10:22, usually translated as "peacock"). This might have been corrupted into "turkey," and thus first introduced to the English-speaking world.

Disappointed yet still hopeful, Columbus set sail a second time from Spain in September 1493. Once more the expenses necessary for his trip were furnished by the confiscated wealth of the Jews. All the precious metals, gold and silver utensils, jewels, gems entrusted by the fleeing Jews for safe keeping to Marrano relatives or "unlawfully" taken by Christians were to be "lawfully" taken over by officials of the large cities of Spain and given to Francisco Pinelo, treasurer of Seville, for the purpose of the voyage. At least six million maravedis were thus obtained, including the ten thousand maravedis paid to Columbus for being the first to sight land.

This time he had a fleet of seventeen vessels, carrying fifteen hundred men, horses, cattle, sheep, hogs, chickens, fruit and vegetables, seeds and sugar cane from the Canaries. He established the colony of Isabella on the island of Haiti—the first permanent settlement of Europeans in the Western Hemisphere.

Of his subsequent trips along the northern coast of South America, of his efforts to find a passage to Asia further west, of the year during which he skirted the savage shores of Central America from Nicaragua to Panama, we shall not speak here. Nor shall we speak of the misfortunes which befell "the Admiral of the Mosquitoes," as he was called by the court wits. Nor is there any point in repeating that the man whose vision and courage and determination discovered a new world was not even to have the honor of giving it his name. There is no parallelism of merit and reward. Many a Moses, major and minor, has not been allowed to enter the promised land for which he gave his life.

Nor is it of any moment to say that other Europeans had reached these shores long before Columbus. The Norse Vikings, it is true, had sailed from Scandinavia to Greenland, where a settlement existed in the tenth century. Leif the Lucky, son of Eric the Red, came from Iceland to our shores, somewhere between Labrador and Cape Cod, in the year 1000. He is reputed to have found a pleasant country abounding in wild grapes, for which reason he called it "Vineland the Good." Doubtless other sailors, braving the awful dangers of the Atlantic—or the Ocean Sea, as it was called—the monsters, the griffons, the dreaded worm which bored through hulls, the mountains of loadstone which drew the iron spikes from planks, and above all Satan himself, who swallowed sailors and boats and vomited them into the fires of hell, took a chance and sailed on until they reached land. Perhaps they even returned to tell tall tales about strange people and strange animals, but they were considered madmen, atheists, or mere liars. At any rate, America, as Mark Twain said, "did not stay discovered," and success is the only valid gauge humans accept.

It was not the fault of the men. It was neither their lack

of courage nor their lack of intelligence. It was an open secret among the more educated seamen that the earth was round; a sort of magnetic needle was in use, sub rosa or otherwise, centuries before the birth of Columbus; the astrolabe, a device for calculating the altitude of stars and measuring latitude, was already perfected a century previously; "Portolani" or "Port-Charts" were numerous and as early as 1339 one showed the shores of the Mediterranean with absolute exactness.

But the time had not yet come. "To everything there is a season, and a time to every purpose under the heaven." A sea of darkness had engulfed Europe for century after century.

There were façades of civilization—a cathedral, a learned monk illuminating an ancient volume, an artist painting the Madonna and the saints, a pageant in which princes of state and church rustled in silks and glowed in gems—but the inner structure was foul with crass ignorance, complete illiteracy, coarseness, penury, cruelty, hopelessness, wretched hovels and stinking streets, populations decimated by wars and plagues, a life expectancy of twenty-five years, terror of devils and hell and a wilder terror still of intelligence and enlightenment and invention.

The Crusades, too, so fulsomely vaunted, caused such carnage and devastation that the introduction of chivalry and spices of which poets and their patrons speak adds but mockery to the vast tragedy. Moreover, the Christian world was held in such contempt by the Asiatics that finally the Ottoman Turks dared to challenge it and nearly succeeded in destroying it. And whether 1453, the date in which the great city of Constantinople fell into their hands, may be considered the beginning of the new era, is rather pointless. New eras do not start, like well-regulated trains, at specified moments. They germinate for long periods; they break out at many points; they gather momentum; and when they are in bloom one may know the many roots, but not *the* root, and the many dates, but not *the* date.

Certain it is that things were happening—the invention of paper and the printing press, the formation of national states, the decadence of feudalism, the multiplication of "communes" or towns, the clipping of the papal power, the advent of gunpowder, making the peasant the equal of the nobleman, and a variety of other desirable matters, and the Dark Sea receded, receded, and there was a rebirth—a renaissance—culminating for our purposes in the discovery of the New World by Christopher Columbus.

It may be argued that Columbus did not seek a new world, but was a greedy and ambitious man in the employ of greedy and ambitious men, that he was unaware to the end of his miserable days that between Europe and India there was not only the Atlantic Ocean but a vast continent and a vaster ocean beyond that continent, and that, therefore, he must be ruled out as an insignificant explorer and a later man, who was aware of the situation, be taken as the culminating point.

But the secret or avowed purposes of men often have very little relation to their accomplishments, and often evil is the fertilizer essential to the blossoming of good. Virtue is its own reward or else vice triumphs doubly.

Columbus proved to the world that the Atlantic could be crossed and re-crossed. He freed the world from the incubus of fear of the Ocean. He established the fact that there were human beings beyond the Ocean with whom one could have business and cultural intercourse. In short, Columbus had blazed the path. It was much easier after that to convince queens and governments and owners of boats that there *were* "worlds to conquer." It was only a question of a few years before it became apparent, indeed, that a new world had been discovered. In 1507, as a matter of fact, barely fifteen years after Columbus had set sail from Palos in his tiny fleet, Martin Waldseemüller, an insignificant professor in the little college of San Dié in the Vosges Mountains, said, in a new edition of the *Geography of Ptolemy*, that "another fourth part of the world has been discovered by Americus Vespucci . . . [the Florentine merchant who helped fit out Columbus' expedition and who had made a voyage of discovery in 1501, reaching the coast of Brazil, and bragging about "the new world" in his letters without really understanding the significance of his words]. I do not see what fairly hinders us from calling it Amerige or America, viz., the land of Americus."

Columbus had already been dead for a year and his heart could not break a second time.

Great explorers followed, many colonizations took place, the waters of destiny flowed fast and furiously under many bridges, but we must return to our Empire State and the great river, as yet unnamed by white man, and resume our tale.

5 The White Man Cometh

WHAT white man first laid eyes upon the Hudson? Was it Amasis, one of the Magi, as the Dutch legend claims? Somehow, he found his way to this side of the great ocean. Scandalized to see the natives worship the Sun, Giver of Light and Life, he built his own altar upon the summit of High Tor and worshiped his own god. Who was his own god? Was it Jesus of Nazareth? He had anticipated His birth and had paid Him a flying visit in the manger. Had he also anticipated His divinity? Or did the Magus, perchance, live as long as Methuselah?

It could hardly have been Guatama, the Buddha, to whom the Magus prayed, for the Enlightened One denied any ritualism and insisted upon the necessity of pity, kindliness, and patience, for which he has properly been called an atheist. Had the Magus followed these precepts the Indians would have welcomed him as a brother, but he enraged them by his sacerdotal ways and they rose in rebellion against him, stormed the mountain, and were on the point of smashing the altar and releasing his spirit from the bondage of the flesh. But a miracle ensued. An earthquake cleft the mountain, swallowed his enemies, and opened the channel through which the Hudson started its career with a paean to the mysterious god of the Magus, who freed it from the evil spirits which had held it imprisoned among the rocks for a billion years.

And after the Magus? Was it John Cabot in 1498? He seems to have followed the western shores of the Atlantic as far as Florida. If so, he was within the reach of a short turn into the mouth of the river. Had he made the turn?

Giovanni da Verrazzano, the Florentine, in 1524 undertook a voyage of exploration for King Francis of France. He crossed the Atlantic near Florida, then traveled up the coast and returned to France. From Dieppe, he wrote a letter to his boss, "his most serene and Christian Majesty."

At the end of a hundred leagues we found a very agreeable situation located within two small prominent hills, in the midst of which flowed to the sea a very great river, which was deep within the mouth; and from the sea to the hills of that place with the rising of the tides, which we found eight feet, any laden ship might have passed. . . . We were with the Dauphin's one small boat, entering the said river to the land, which we found much populated. The people . . . clothed with the feathers of birds of various colors, came to us joyfully, uttering very great exclamations of admiration, showing us where we could land with the boat more safely. . . .

In an instant, as is wont to happen in navigation a gale of unfavorable wind blowing from the sea, we were forced to return to the ship, leaving the said land with much regret because of its commodiousness and beauty thinking it was not without some properties of value, all of its hills showing indications of minerals.

If the gale had not risen, would Verrazzano have sailed on that "very great river"? Would it have been called now the Verrazzano River in honor of its first European explorer? He was in search of a shorter route to old Cathay, while a new Cathay far wealthier and far more fabulous confronted him. How should be know? How shall man know the present if he does not know the future—the present which forever flows into the past, the future which forever eludes him? Thus, between the anvil of the past and the hammer of the future, the present is mangled and beaten out of shape.

But what price wisdom if it can only discourse on the things that are no more and console us of misfortunes not our own? Said the Owl:

> I foretold the death of many,
> But one second before my own occurred,
> I closed my eyes and thought
> Of a nest of little mice
> And the bounty of the God of Owls.
> What is wisdom if it cannot teach you
> When to spread your wings and fly;
> If it cannot hinder your becoming
> A stuffed owl glaring out of glass beads?

Verrazzano was followed by Estavan Gomez, a Portuguese sailor in the service of Spain. With the gold and jewels stolen from the Jews driven penniless to all the four winds and into the waves of the seas, Spain was more than ever bent upon becoming the greatest empire in history. If she never became the greatest, she certainly was the cruelest. Wherever her cavaliers went there also went the sacred bishops of the Holy Office of the Inquisition, and wherever they settled civilizations died in blood and flames.

Gomez had already made several voyages to the West Indies and had accompanied Magellan to the Straits. He had seen the Hudson and even took the trouble to baptize it Río San Antonio (also called by the Spaniards of the day Río de Guamas and Río de Gomez), but had he sailed upon it?

Ribero stated in 1527 that the stretch of land afterward known as Rhode Island and Maryland was charted as Tierra de Esteva Gomez, but the mariner himself had, as far as it is known, left no account of his voyage. Therefore we must conclude that the virginal waters of the Hudson had not yet been ravished by an explorer from *Outre-Mer*.

The Spaniards were followed by the French, who even traded with the Indians, so the Dutch stated, claiming also that the French had been the discoverers of the river and "proving" it by a well-annotated map. That was in 1614 and it was calculated to offset the English claim that one of theirs had first plunged oar into the River-with-many-names. It was a manner of cutting off one's nose to spite one's face. But France was the weaker of Holland's enemies and by contrast might be called friend. The time was to come when England would be Holland's friend, but in international politics friends change positions with foes as partners do in quadrilles.

There were other maps at the time which traced the course of the river at least as far as the junction with the Mohawk, the two most famous being Gastaldi's of Venice and the Mercator of Duisberg.

They were all still chasing the will o' the wisp—a short route to the Indies *via* the New World, and get-rich-quick. Always alchemy and astrology. Man has no time. He must beat nature and discover his fate before fate overtakes him. And what a price he pays for gold and for knowledge!

Impoverished by the endless wars with Spain, which almost wiped her off the map, the Dutch wished speedily to recoup their losses. "India! India!" all shouted. Alas, for India. The time was to come when she would curse all the roads that ever led to her door and all the feet that landed upon her shore.

And so the Dutch looked around for the right man to take her to India the easy way. There were stalwart mariners among her sons. After all, Holland is really beneath the waters of the seas and, in a sense, a land of fish—human fish, meaning no disrespect either to the Dutch or to the fish. But the Dutch always had a great admiration for foreigners, and truth to tell, often were kindlier to them than all the other nations of Europe. The Spanish and Portuguese Jews, for instance, and later the Puritans had good reason to be grateful to that nation of canals and dykes and bridges.

Henry Hudson—that was the man. Every inch of him a Captain. What had he done to deserve his reputation? Well, he had made two voyages for England, his native country: one in 1607 which landed him in Greenland and Iceland, the second, a year later, which brought him as far as Nova Zembla, where ice forced him to return. But did he find the milky way to the land of jewels and silks? That he did not, luckily. Or else, would he still have been available? But if he did not find it for England, would he find it for Holland? Three is a lucky number. The third trip will do it. Henry Hudson. We want Henry Hudson! But if he finds the route, would he not claim it for England? Is he not an Englishman above all things? What naiveté! *Ubi bene ibi patria.* The *purse* determined a man's nationality.

And so it happened that on April 4, 1609, Henry (or Hendrick, as the good burghers of Old Amsterdam affectionately called him) Hudson set sail on *De Holve Maene—The Half-Moon*—a small vessel, a "yacht" of eighty tons burden, with a length of fifty-eight feet, maximum breadth of sixteen and a draft of about seven. The interior had a hold, a 'tween deck, an upper-deck, and a poop-deck above the captain's cabin.

There were eighteen or twenty men in the crew, partly Dutch, partly English, always quarreling. Their names seem to have been written in the wind, except two—John Hudson, the Captain's son, and Robert Juet, who immortalized himself by writing the narrative of the voyage. It was little enough for such coveted reward, considering the thousands of writers and the millions of books vanished without leaving more sign or clue of their existence than the *neiges d'antan*. Though why man should worry about his immortal name when his flesh is mortal is something about which many have written but none made clear.

After eight weeks at sea, the crew of the *Half-Moon* sighted land, somewhere in Nova Scotia probably, and on July 18 anchored in some harbor on the Maine coast. On August 6 they reached Cape Cod and steered to the southwest, entered Delaware Bay on August 28, continued north, and on September 3 entered what was destined to become New York Bay, anchoring at Sandy Hook. "This is a very good land to fall with and a pleasant land to see," wrote Juet in his notebook. On September 4 they sent out a boat to fish and the men brought in a prize catch of ten mullets and a ray requiring four men to haul—doubtless the first fish story told by a white man on this continent.

For nine days the mariners reconnoitered the bay, slowly made their way up the narrows, and anchored across what is now 110th Street, Manhattan.

Some of the River Indians had taken the beautiful ship for a giant fish sent by Manitou to devour them for the evil deeds they had committed, man's conscience always being a little muddy. Others considered it a great white bird sent by the Sun, the god of light, and made ready to worship it, man's knees being rather weak. Nor should the gods be over-vain, for he who kneels today kicks tomorrow, and those raised on pedestals are sooner or later buried underneath them.

However, the more sensible of the Indians regained their equilibrium and, clad in deerskins and feather mantles as a sign of respect, ventured aboard, bringing with them gifts

of big green leaves of tobacco, maize, and corn bread. The
bread the sailors ate, both cheeks full, for their teeth were
good and their appetites healthy. As for the leaves of tobacco, they probably imitated their guests, rolled them, lit
them, puffed and coughed and laughed, even as children do
when they manufacture cigars out of newspapers. And when
they laughed, doubtless they were joined by the natives, and
the natives knew that these strange beings who had arrived
in the giant fish were human, for laughter is the human shib-
boleth.

And after laughter—barter, since man is bored with what
he has and covets his neighbor's possessions. And so they
were anxious to trade grain and fruit and furs for trinkets
and tools or, if trade they could not, steal a little. Master
Hudson found these simple people "exceedingly adroit in
carrying away whatever they took a fancy to."

The next day the sailors went ashore, wrote Juet:

and saw great store of Men, Women and Children, who gave
them tobacco at their coming on land. So they went up into the
Woods, and saw great store of very goodly Oakes, and some
Currents. For one of them came aboard and brought some dryed,
and gave me some, which were sweet and good. This day many
of the people came aboard, some in Mantles of Feathers, and
some in Skinnes of divers sorts of good Furres. Some of the
Women also came to us with Hempe. They had red Copper Tobacco pipes, and other things of Copper they did wear about
their neckes.

Which of the two vipers stings the breast of man first—
hate or fear? But this is certain, that when one implants its
poison, the other follows suit, and thereafter the heart pulses
fear - hate - hate - fear - fear - hate — maniac diastolic - systolic
rhythm.

Suddenly the seamen became apprehensive. While the sun

was up the white man and the red man had been friends. But ". . . at night, the Indians went on Land againe, so wee rode very quiet, but durst not trust them."

The day after, as a small boat party was on its way back to the *Half-Moon*, the Indians sent an arrow through a sailor's neck and killed him. And on the twelfth of September "there came eight and twenty canoes full of men, women and children, to betray us: but we saw their intent, and suffered none of them to come aboard of us. At twelve of the clocke they departed."

Strange faces cast shadows which chill the marrow and strange tongues strike the ear like tolling bells.

But Captain Hudson would not be intimidated nor would he snub the inhabitants. Without escort except a native, he went ashore, and his courage and confidence were antidotes to fear and hate. He relates the incident in his own diary:

I sailed to the shore in one of their canoes, with an old man, who was the chief of the tribe consisting of forty men and seventeen women; these I saw there in a house well constructed of oak bark and circular in shape. On our coming into the house, two mats were spread out to sit upon, and immediately some food was served in well made red wooden bowls; two men were also despatched at once with bows and arrows in quest of game, who soon after brought in a pair of pigeons. They likewise killed at once a fat dog and skinned it in great haste with shells which they got out of the water. They supposed I would remain for the night, but I returned after a short time on board the ship. . . . The natives are a very good people; for, when they saw that I would not remain, they supposed that I was afraid of their bows, and taking the arrows, they broke them in pieces, and threw them into the fire. . . .

Goaded by the distrust of his men, however, Master Hudson evidently accepted their challenge to prove whether the chiefe men of the Countrey . . . had any treacherie in them, [writes Juet]. So they took into the Cabbin, and gave them so much wine and Aqua Vitae, that they were all merrie; and one of them had his wife with him, which sate so modestly, as any of our Countrey women would doe in a strange place. In the end one of them was drunke, which had been aboard of our ship all the time . . . and that was strange to them; for they could not tell how to take it. So he slept all night quietly. When the people of the Countrey came and saw the Savages well, they were glad.

The mariners strutted and swaggered and guffawed, pointing forefingers to sacred things which seemed ludicrous to them. And, too, with the legerdemain of sea-faring folk, they stole an article here and there to bring back to mistress and wife. Their chronicler does not mention this, but what sailor in the seventeenth century was not part marauder? Moreover, Juet does state that they had stolen two natives, whom they intended to take home as slaves. The natives managed to escape and wriggle their thumbs at their would-be captors, or a gesture to that effect. Small wonder, then, that:

This afternoone, one Canoe kept hanging under sterne with one man in it. . . . [he] stole out my Pillow, and two Shirts, and two Bandleeres. Our Masters Mate shot at him, and strooke him in on the brest, and killed him. . . . We manned our Boate, and got our things againe. When one of them . . . got hold of our Boate, our Cooke tooke a Sword, and cut off one of his hands, and he was drowned.

Fear and hate—hate and fear—and now the ancient sachem began to mumble to himself the legend which recounted how their ancestors had been driven out of their homes by pale-faced foes who made them weary wanderers until they reached "the-stream-that-flows-both-ways." And he further mumbled, as he moved his copper pipe from one side of his mouth to the other: "Since when do eagles catch flies?"

The stalwart of the tribe understood:

Two Canoes full of men with Bowes and Arrowes shot at us after our sterne; in recompense whereof we discharged sixe Muskets, and killed two or three of them. Then above a hundred of them came to a point of Land to shoot at us. There I shot a Falcon at them, and killed two of them. . . . They manned off another Canoe with nine or ten men, which came to meet us. So I shot at it also a Falcon, and shot it through, and killed one of them. Then our Men with their Muskets killed three or foure of them. So they went their way. . . .

On October 4, weather and wind being fair, the crew weighed anchor. "By twelve of the clocke," Juet writes, "We were cleere of all the inlet. Then we took in our Boate, and set Mayne-sayle and sprit-sayle, and our top-sayles, and steered away East Southeast, and Southeast by East off in the mayne sea."

The *Half-Moon* was once more on the Atlantic, and the natives licked their wounds but breathed freely. They danced around their totem-poles and sang the song of liberation. It *was* an evil bird, some reminded the others who had not hearkened to them; it *was* the spirits of their ancient enemies once again incarnated; it *was* punishment for evil deeds. Be that as it might, the nightmare was over, and one could live again.

How little they knew the white man. The white man is persistent, if he is anything, and always finds pious and pompous reasons why he is entitled to despoil and decimate those who have not weapons or craftiness equal to his. He invokes God, Father of all men, and Truth, which maketh free, and Justice blindfolded that she may see neither the color of gold nor the color of skin, and never does he embroider upon his banners: "For Injustice and Falsehood and Greed."

But the ancient sachem mourned the dead of his tribe and prayed to the spirits of the waters to sink all boats of the pale-faced invaders, and mumbled warnings. "The tiger kisses the flesh he has torn before he devours it. Soft is the paw of the wolf that comes to steal the papoose. Honeyed is the tongue of the foe. Anger sharpens the teeth."

Henry Hudson could not say with the Roman: "I have reared a monument more lasting than brass," for he was only aware of his frustration. Perhaps he thought of Columbus and his tragedy. Columbus went in search of a continent and discovered an ocean. He himself had gone in search of an ocean and found only a continent. Perhaps he said, "Alas, my name and my fame are writ in water." And Neptune, god of all the seas, shook his trident, and roared with laughter, for he knows that nothing, not rock nor any metal man scoops out of rock, nor anything he sculpts or carves or raises, however high, however formidable, can outlast water. In the beginning there was water and water shall be in the end, and there shall be nothing else.

And while the Master of the *Half-Moon* was plunged in despair, what mighty curses shot out of the throats of the crew in English and Dutch and who knows in what other languages which they had picked up at the many ports they had landed. The first words man learns of a foreign tongue and the last he forgets are the maledictions, for he never finds enough to express his anger, his disdain, his hate.

To forget, they filled their tankards.

"Master Henry, drink with us! Drink with us!" The oldest offered him the cup.

His throat was shut with grief and shame. Three times

now he was proven a fool and an ignoramus. He shook his
head.

"Drink, father," John prayed.

"Drink, Master!"

"Thank you, men," he finally accepted.

Soon they roared with laughter, for what in all Cathay
could be half as delicious or half as precious as the seething
cateract which tumbled into their bellies?

A general may die in bed, but what captain of the sea
does not prefer the wave to the grave? And Henry Hudson
set sail a fourth time in 1610. This time he tried a more
northerly route and reached the Bay that now bears his
name. With eight companions he put into a small boat and
set adrift, and was nevermore seen or heard of—in human
shape—but is seen and heard in all time in the shape of a
great River.

What is man, if not a river—with tides and waves and
myriad tributaries—forever pulled upward by the magnet of
his dream, as by a luminous moon, but forever incapable of
tearing himself from the shores of his skin? And every river
of a man some day freezes—main branch and tributaries—
the tides stilled and the dream which was the luminous moon
darkened—an anonymous drop tumbling into the vast Sea
Of Nothingness.

6 Geese Have Their Fat Points

THE merchants who had invested their shiny florins in the Henry Hudson expeditions were downcast. Some were on the verge of bankruptcy; others would have to relinquish their social status, and that was a misfortune equal to death.

"What fools we were to allow ourselves to be deceived by Hudson's words and appearance!"

"I warned you, didn't I?"

"Everybody warned everybody else, and everybody invested."

"We were all fools. Let's acknowledge that."

"And now we shall all be paupers. Let's acknowledge that, too."

"There is no parallelism between foolishness and pauperism. Indeed, I have often noticed the reverse."

"We all thank you for your bit of cynicism, Mijnheer David de Sola."

"Only a bit of truth, gentlemen," de Sola smiled faintly. He was tall, swarthy, long-faced—a poet's rather than a merchant's face, and particularly striking among the ruddy, heavy-jowled individuals sitting at the round table. "You have but to look in the marketplace and at the bourse, and you will almost come to the conclusion that God has a special fondness for fools and guides their steps, while the rest of us

63

—well, we must shift for ourselves, sometimes with disastrous results."

"Mijnheer de Sola has at least the kindness to include us among the less favored of God."

"Gentlemen," de Sola ignored the remark. "Swans may be more beautiful than geese, but geese have their fat points."

"He cannot get over his swampy origin—geese," one of the men made a wry face.

De Sola heard but pretended deafness. He had learned from his father, that "a stuffed ear avoids cyclones." Had he wished, however, he could have told the corpulent burgher, whose pointed, square nose suggested a goose's beak (for which reason, perhaps unconsciously he had resented the Jew's remark), that his grandfather had the highest title short of royal blood in Spain, and that, indeed, he had been among the favorites at the Court. But the envy of other courtiers and the greed of the Holy Office of the Inquisition, caused his ruin and his death. He was accused of being a Marrano, of celebrating the Passover in secret, and was tortured and burned at the stake; his vast estates were confiscated. His eldest son succeeded in running away to Holland with a bag of jewels. He had been a devout Catholic. Now he had himself circumcized and returned to the religion of his ancestors. His own son was a devout Jew and, following the tradition of his race, became a scholar before entering the mercantile life. Now, in his middle age, he was one of the richest of Amsterdam's burghers.

"And where are the geese with the fat points?" one asked sarcastically.

"Haven't you seen the furs Hudson's sailors brought from —let us call it the New World, until we learn precisely what it is."

"Feathers, I should think, would have been more apropos."

"I am interested in diamonds—and the mountains to dig them."

De Sola cut the chatter short. "With the right sort of shovel pelts are also mountains. I am ready to invest my florins. Are you, gentlemen?"

And so it happened that although Henry Hudson did not report to the merchants of Amsterdam the great news that he had planted the flag of Holland in the heart of Cathay, or that he had filled the hold of the *Half-Moon* with precious stones, the shrewd and hardy men of the country which has to raise itself out of the briny sea by its own bootstraps, settled "on geese and their fat points."

One year after the Hudson "fiasco," the Dutch merchants sent a ship to the high walled valley which the English explorer had claimed for them and obtained soon after, from the High and Mighty Lords of the States-General, a grant to resort and trade exclusively in these parts, for which they paid the required sum, plus who knows what little gifts. They added, besides, a note of patriotism in the transaction, for they proposed (and it was accepted) that the name of the "Great River of the Mountains," as it was called impersonally by its discoverer, should henceforth and into all eternity be called the "River of the Prince Mauritius," in honor of their mighty soldier, Maurice of Orange.

The merchants in 1615 "built on the North River, about the Island Manhattans, a redoubt or little fort, wherein was left a small garrison, some people usually remaining there to carry on trade with the natives or Indians. This was continued and maintained until their High Mightinesses did in the year 1622 include this country of New Netherland in the charter of the West India Company," writes an historian of the period.

Meanwhile the Dutch East India Company chose to ignore or ridicule the grant given the new association which read in part:

Whereas we understand it would be honorable, serviceable and profitable to this country, and for the promotion of its prosperity, as well as for the maintenance of seafaring people, that the good inhabitants should be excited and encouraged to employ and occupy themselves in seeking out and discovering passages, havens, countries and places . . . and being informed by some traders that they intended with God's merciful help, by diligence, labor, danger and expense, to employ themselves thereat, as they expect to derive a handsome profit therefrom.

But the people who ventured across the ocean were not particularly anxious to transfer their homes permanently to this part of the world. There was, indeed, no real urgency—neither political nor religious—similar to that which had driven the Puritans and the Quakers to seek after habitations, nor was there economic depression. They went abroad to trade, to "derive a handsome profit," and then return to their native cities to spend and live above the stratum of society in which they had been before they had left. For after all, what's the fun in becoming rich if those who disbelieved in you, or those who held you in contempt, can't see you in all your glory?

But even the first shipload of colonists was not composed exclusively of Hollanders. Indeed, for the entire half-century of the Dutch political control of the River, the colonists were, as recorded by Father Isaac Jogues, in 1643, "of 18 different languages." There were Swedes, Germans, Irish, Danes, Englishmen, Walloons, and the New Amsterdam preacher Megapolensis complained bitterly of the influx of Jewish immigrants, requesting "that the godless rascals . . . may be sent away from here."

This conglomeration of nationalities foreshadowed the future of our country much more accurately than did the New England colonies which were far more uniform in social and domestic habits, in law and in language.

The River Indians had forgotten or discounted the first encounter with the whites and now welcomed them. They had been in the throes of perpetual war with their stronger brethren, the Iroquois, and were living in constant terror of being scalped, exterminated, or carried off. They had, in a sense, struck the bottom of misery and saw in the arrival of the Dutch a possible ally. Optimism is the child of despair.

For a while the relation between the Indians and the whites was rather cordial. They did business, bartering furs for trinkets and, alas, for rum. Only later, as it became quite clear that the pale-faced strangers from beyond the waters had all the intentions of taking their lands "for keeps," did the Indians begin to retaliate. It became no longer a struggle of supremacy among the various tribes but a holy war of all against the intruder.

The traders who came to the New World were not cast into impenetrable forests. The Indian had cleared many a pathway. The Great Central Trail crossed from Albany to Lake Erie, the Susquehanna Trail from Albany to the Susquehanna River and into Pennsylvania, from Catskill on the Hudson the trail wound north to another that followed Schoharie Creek and joined the Mohawk. Others, still, led into the North Country from Lake Champlain and the upper Hudson and along the Black River.

The early settlers whose legs were strong and wills stronger still could wend their way from one settlement to

another, and keep in touch with both their friends and their
foes. But rarely were these walks for mere pleasure or adventure. On their backs they carried their merchandise to sell
or barter. Nothing is so strong and enduring as the human
back.

To the West the Great Lakes gave the more intrepid itin-
erants an excellent means of communication, and our step-
father, the Indian, further bequeathed unto us his riches—the
light canoe which, easily toted, proved most suitable between
watersheds and upon the smaller rivers.

But the chief artery, the very heart of travel and trade, was
the Hudson (and the Mohawk, its chief tributary). There
were, later on when business developed, other rivers and
lakes which, even if secondary in their importance, aided the
growth of the State—the Raquette, Oswego, Black, and Genesee which flow into Lake Ontario. There are the Delaware
and the Susquehanna rivers and their tributaries. In the central part of the State there are a number of long, narrow
bodies of water named, because of their shape, "The Finger
Lakes." And there is the St. Lawrence River with its Thousand Islands.

The fur trade grew and, as David de Sola predicted, merchants were beginning to transmute fleas into gems. And
now there was need of a more solid government and of bases
at various points along the River where one could transact
business. With this in mind, the Dutch merchants who had
a controlling influence established the West India Company
in 1621.

The Company was vested with extraordinary powers and
almost exclusive authority, for twenty-four years, subject to
renewal, over the "barbarous coasts" of Africa and America.
A Council of Nineteen, with five city chambers or boards,

was entrusted with the management. The American affairs, however, were the function of the Amsterdam Chamber.

The Charter bound the Company "to advance the peopling of those fruitful and unsettled parts, and to do all that the service of those countries and the profit and increase of trade shall require."

But it was not an easy task to colonize. There was desperate need of farmers and craftsmen. But why should farmers and craftsmen leave a good country, probably the freest in the whole world, and come to the shore of a river surrounded by mountains which sheltered not only savage red-skinned men but also lions, bears, elks, and "other wild animals . . . unknown to Christians."

The province was named New Netherland and was dignified by the armorial insignia of a countship—a beaver surmounted by a count's coronet encircled with the words: *Sigillum Novi Belgii,* "Seal of New Belgium," reminding us that at that time the Lowlands had not yet split up into two kingdoms.

The first boatload, composed of thirty Walloon families, set sail under the captainship of Cornelis Jacobsen May. They arrived in the nick of time to abort the attempt of the commander of a French vessel to appropriate Manhattan in the name of King of France. A Dutch sloop escorted the would-be masters down the bay and politely, but very firmly, requested them to return whence they had come, which they did, seeing that among the decorations of the sloop there were two cannon.

Thereupon the little company from Holland sailed on upon the Great River until they reached the foot of a hill on which, as a minor Rome, Albany would be built. Meanwhile, however, they "built and completed a fort called Orange."

More boats followed with livestocks—each named according to its cargo: *Horse, Sheep, Cow.* There was also a yacht among them, *Mackerel,* which held not the glittering denizen of fresh waters, however, but more colonists. The animals were landed first at Noten Island (later called Governor's Island), but pasture was lacking, and they were taken to Manhattan, where the grass was "as fine and long as one could wish."

7 The Great Bargain

IN 1626 Peter Minuit arrived as director general. Three weeks later he called the Chiefs of the Indians and transacted the first bit of real estate business in the New World. For the sum of sixty guilders, or about twenty-four dollars, paid in trinkets and aqua vitae, which created a thirst nevermore to be slaked until the red race almost disappeared from the face of the Earth, he acquired 22,000 acres on Manhattan, ten acres for a cent.

Were the Indians tricked or did they laugh up their sleeves at the foolishness of the white man? In all our dealings, it is profitable to remember that we are not the only scoundrels. However, the truly remarkable thing is that the Christian gentleman, in this unique instance, actually deigned to *buy* the land from the native, and even took the trouble of drawing up a contract. That is decidedly not his way. The white man's burden does not include the parchment. He *grabs* and carries off. Ask one billion people of various shades of skins all over the afflicted globe.

But now the settlement of Manhattan began in earnest. Thirty cabins "of the bark of trees" were built "on the east side of the river," and families were brought from Orange and Fort Nassau. Besides, a fort was "staked out" for security and called "Fort Amsterdam," while the trading-post was named "New Amsterdam."

Fort Amsterdam was a pompous name for what at no time

was an actual defense or a fort. Before one wall was finished the other crumbled, as if the dwarfs, who afterward met Rip Van Winkle, angry because they were not consulted, were taking revenge. As late as 1647, Peter Stuyvesant, the seventh governor-general, said that it resembled "more a mole hill than a fortress, without gates, the walls and bastions trodden under foot by men and cattle." In 1650 the "Fortress" did not have "one gun carriage or one piece of cannon in a suitable frame or on a good platform." In 1664 whatever there was of it was much too weak to withstand the English men-of-war which arrived in the harbor.

Governor Minuit began his systematic administration—which, generally speaking, meant treating the people as servants in the Company. They could not hold land in their own name, could not engage in manufacturing or deals with the Indians except as the Company's agents.

By 1628 the number of inhabitants had reached 270. Disappointed in their efforts to recruit settlers, the West India Company tried to entice its members by offering them benefits in the rich new land and established the "Charter of Freedoms and Exemptions." Grandiose in promise, in practice it became the Patroon System, with all its vicious implications.

The Charter offered large river estates to all those who within four years of the signing of the contract, would establish settlements of at least fifty persons on the lands granted them. The patroonship might extend along one shore of the river for sixteen miles, or on both shores for eight miles each. and "as far inland as the situations of the occupyers will permit."

There were still further extensions of freedoms granted in 1640 in order to make conditions and opportunities for settlement along the river more enticing. True, the patroon had to buy the land from the Indians, but that bit of formality over he might hold his property as a "perpetual fief of inherit-ance." He did not have to pay duties for eight years and his tenants for ten.

The patroon was the sovereign of his own estate. He was empowered

to administer civil and criminal justice, in person, or by deputy, within his colonie, to appoint local officers and magistrates; to erect courts; to keep a gallows, if such were required, for the execution of malefactors, subject, however, to the restriction that if such gallows, happened, by any accident to fall, pending an execution, a new one could not be erected, unless for the pur-pose of hanging another criminal.

The *Scherprecter*, the hangman, was an official of recognized standing.

There was, as usual in human affairs, the fly in the oint-ment. The patroon might traffic in all things except in furs. This was the sole perquisite of the West India Company. But furs were the gold nuggets of the day, as the tulip bulbs were to be two centuries later for the Netherlanders. As values in Virginia and Maryland were computed in terms of tobacco, so along the Hudson they were reckoned on the basis of pelts. Although wampum and seawan were among the means of exchange, and "tokens stamped by the church" also had limited currency, furs were the chief money.

Who can doubt that, in the circumstances, the black mar-ket flourished? But the chiefs of the Company who shipped home annually between 30,000 and 40,000 pelts, had sense enough to permit a certain amount of aberration. After all, why have two eyes if you can't close one upon occasion, or two hands if you can't let one have a little life all its own?

In the Low Countries the River colony was a sort of stock exchange, Wall Street anticipated by a century and a half.

Everybody invested, everybody gambled, some became wealthy, many lost their shirts, as in Wall Street. It was rarely stivers and florins and guilders that were exchanged, but goods. The New World was starved for necessities, the Old World for luxuries. They were no longer thinking, however, of India and Cathay, of rare silks and embroideries and lapis-lazuli, but of furs—an atavistic yearning to be an innocent beast again, a beaver, a raccoon, a fox, a bear, a wolf. But no fur was needed to become a hog.

The Hudson played the chief role in this commerce. The *vlie booten,* the flyboats, from Holland came to the mouth of the River, anchored, and disembarked cargoes of every variety of goods—implements needed for farming, clothing, candles, linen, woolens, cotton cloths, for looms were not allowed in the patroonships. What were colonies, anyway, but maws into which to stuff the goods made in the dear homeland? Sooner or later there was bound to be indigestion, sooner or later the colonists would claim that they, too, had the right to manufacture what they pleased, to sell whatever was profitable—and there would be riots and revolutions. Could not the masters foresee this? Could not the wise men of parliaments? To what use history? Who does not kill the hen that lays the golden egg?

Perhaps the first of the maps drawn during that period (a nightmare of inaccuracies, showing "River of the Prince Mauritius," a maniacal stream breaking through hellish caverns) already had the names of settlements destined to become important in the history of the River—Nassau (Albany), Kinderhook, Esopus, Tappan.

Cultivation spread slowly to the forest lands. The pine and the chestnut, mighty trees, surrendered to the dainty wheat and the hairy corn and the clinging vine from which hung, like fragrant breasts, grapes white and blue and deep red.

"Their juice is very pleasant," says a report issued by Their Mightinesses, the States-General, "and some of it like French or Rhenish wines . . . and others like Tent."

There were those, of course, who preferred the more somnolent of the daughters of Bacchus, and some of the *bouweries* raised hops. And how could the sentimental *vrouw* not plant flowers—roses to remind her of her love, tulips to remind her of her home? But the surrounding wilderness did not give up without a struggle. Many a *bouwerie* was reabsorbed, and more than once the dwellers of the forest, man and beast, reassumed supremacy. But the beast, as usually, was the more clement.

The pendulum which had started in the days of Henry Hudson to swing between hate and fear, began once more its malevolent rhythm, more vigorously now and more persistently, since the Indians could not but realize that henceforth the crafty paleface would nevermore return whence he came. Oh, he was glad to do business with him, to exchange skins of animals for lots of good and pretty things, and particularly for firewater, which turned feet into wings and filled the throats with song, but why did he steal some of his strongest and sell them into slavery in far-off places? Why did the Company's laborers rob and murder an Indian near the pond called "Fresh Water"? Why did Governor Kieft wage war against them for two years, and finally order a general slaughter in February 1643?

Any wonder, then, that (as one old paper of the times writes):

Pacham, a crafty chief, ran through all the villages, urging the Indians to a general massacre. Thereupon it happened that certain Indians called Wappingers, dwelling sixteen leagues up the River, with whom we never had the least trouble, seized a boat coming from Fort Orange, wherein were only two men, and full

four hundred beavers. This great booty stimulated others to follow the example; so that they seized two boats more, intending
to overhaul the fourth also; from which they were driven, with
loss of six Indians. Nine Christians, including two women, were
murdered in these two barks; one woman and two children remaining prisoners. The rest of the Indians, as soon as their maize
was ripe, followed this example; and through semblance of selling
beavers, killed an old man and woman, leaving another man with
five wounds, who, however, fled to the fort, in a boat, with a little
child in his arms, which, in the first outbreak, had lost father and
mother, and now grandfather and grandmother; being thus twice
rescued, through God's merciful blessing, from the hands of the
Indians; first, when two years old. Nothing was now heard but
murders; most of which were committed under the pretence of
coming to put Christians on their guard. Finally, the Indians
took the field and attacked the bouweries at Pavonia. Two ships
of war and a privateer were here at the time, and saved considerable cattle and grain. Probably it was not possible to prevent
the destruction of four bouweries on Pavonia which were burnt;
not by open violence, but by stealthy creeping through the bush
with fire in hand, and in this way igniting the roofs which were
all either of reed or straw; one covered with plank was preserved
at the time.

In 1633 Wouter van Twiller, formerly a clerk in the ware-
house of the West India Company became governor-general.
He was, according to Brodhead, historian of New York, "de-
ficient in the knowledge of men, inexperienced, incompetent
and irresolute." Washington Irving called him "the doubter"
—an enviable appellation, for doubt is the root of all truth.

Nevertheless, he tried to serve his masters in the best way
he knew how. He repaired the "fort" and erected a guard
house and barracks within the enclosure. He set up three
windmills, one of them on Broadway. For himself he built a
brick mansion in conformity with his importance and several

wooden houses for his subordinates. He also erected a bakery, a brewery, a boat-house, and several barns.

Like Minuit, van Twiller did not neglect the spiritual side of his people. Minuit turned the loft over the horse-mill into a church; his successor offered a barn-like structure on Pearl Street to divine functions. And for Domine Bogardus, whom he had brought over, he provided a house and a stable.

But Domine Bogardus had his own opinions about the governor-generals. The Dutch Reformed Church was the state church, he held, and he was going to make it clear to all. He was a cousin-in-spirit to Cotton Mather in another part of the New World. He did not see witches in brooms but he saw heretics in tankards—his own, for he was a great bibber. Ah, the colossal battles he waged with the Governor. Governor Minuit, he said, "was a slippery fellow; under the painted mask of honesty, is a compound of all iniquity and wickedness . . . and the use of horrible oaths and execrations." Governor Van Twiller, he called "a child of Satan" against whom he would preach "such a sermon as will make him shake in his shoes." Later he said about Governor Kieft and his associates: "In Africa which has a climate of intense heat different species of animals come together by which means monsters are generated. But I know not from whence, in such a temperate climate as this, such monsters of men are produced."

Governor Kieft responded by pointing out the differences between certain rites which the Domine conducted when he was "dead drunk" and only "pretty drunk." But no one knew how he would conduct them when sober. To make certain that Domine Bogardus would not be heard thundering his answer from the pulpit, the Governor ordered the Fort Amsterdam drum corps to beat their loudest outside the church during the pastor's services.

It was proclaimed pompously and with pride (which is a cardinal sin) that there was religious liberty in New Netherland. And many came to worship in their own manner, but soon discovered that the church was more generous in words than in deeds, and the best they could hope for was tolerance —of all human emotions the most degrading. But even that was denied the Quakers, because they had the audacity to take seriously the injunction of universal brotherhood, even including the Indian. As for the Jew, as always he had a special treatment accorded him. He could not practice a trade, open a business, nor follow a profession. His rights of locomotion were determined by the governor or an official whose appetite for justice was stimulated by the apéritif concocted of florins and stivers.

Nevertheless, there *was* more religious freedom in New Netherland than in New England. Red noses are more generous than blue.

By dint of courage, intelligence, aggressiveness, and greed the Dutch not only survived but became the dominant factor along the River, and the period between Henry Hudson's exploration and the English conquest was definitely Dutch. All the other settlers, of whatever nationality or tongue, surrendered political control to the Dutch. Moreover, long after New Netherland was only a name the River country continued to feel the influence of its original citizens.

A century and a half later, Washington Irving wrote about these people in his *Knickerbocker History,* to entertain rather than instruct, as he said. But those who entertain instruct, and the caricature became the picture. Who does not know that the Dutch were fatheaded, had great derrières, were forever yawning, spoke with silly pomposity? The truth, however, is that colonists of this type not only could not have survived the hardships of a new and dangerous home but would never have left their comfortable fireplaces and arm-chairs. Only the lean and hungry-faced, the tough, the rough, the roistering, dared challenge the new, the hazardous, the savage. First came the tiger, then the cat. What has the tiger to do with a parlor, except as a skin upon the floor?

A new world is a new jungle, and those who venture into it must have the surviving qualities required in a jungle—fangs and claws and muscles of steel. The early Dutch, as well as the representatives of the other nations, had these requisites. They were hard, lawless, cruel, shrewd, brave. And they knew the motto "every man for himself" and accepted it without sentimental reinterpretation.

Even the games of these frontiersmen would have sent the cultured caballero Washington Irving running for safety. "Clubbing the Cat" and "Pulling the Goose" were among the mildest. For variants, they used rabbits and eels. And what is recorded in the annals of Animaldom against man in general, and our forefathers in particular, it is well for us that we cannot read.

And what a sense of humor they displayed. Firing guns at night and "causing the people to spring out of their beds all at once." Galloping horses through town and howling. Teasing frightened natives. Blowing loud trumpets into the ears of unsuspecting neighbors, terrorizing them.

But man has always lived in glass houses, and it ill becomes any generation to stand in judgment on another. Man never regrets the past sufficiently to reform the future. He is an impatient traveler without destination.

Gradually, the patroonship increased in number and in wealth, and the manor lords had baronial state and power. Not allowed to trade in furs, they switched to lumber and shipbuilding, and how they despoiled the fine forests on the River hills. Centuries were to pass before man's cupidity, if

not his love and wisdom, made him begin to plant new trees
for those felled by his axe.

But even as early as 1631 a ship more than twenty-five
times the tonnage of the *Half-Moon,* one of the largest afloat,
was built in Manhattan. Like so many other ships of the
time, it carried thirty guns for defense against the pirates.
As if to annoy those enamored of the present, countering
Solomon's statement that nothing is new under the sun by
saying that all's new under the sun, camouflage was already
being practised. Boats which were not adequately protected
by guns had false portholes painted upon them from stern
to stern to bluff those pirates who dared not come aboard
and investigate.

8 Shaping Up

FOUR nations had already begun the struggle for the domination of the New World. Spain was solidly planted in the South. Along the Atlantic Coast England, France, and Holland were seeking the elimination of one another. In 1633 the Dutch had bought from the natives the land around Hartford and erected a block-house, the first on the Connecticut River. The Puritans, professedly their friends in memory of the hospitality extended them by the mother country when they had to leave England, would not give up the valley.

An armed vessel left Plymouth, sailed up the river, and defied the Dutch commander at Hartford. Two years of building fortresses and maneuvering found the English masters of both banks of the river and the Dutch block-house cut off. Thus made helpless, the Dutch surrendered to their more powerful rival.

The French, with the help of the Indians, whose friendship they seemed to obtain more easily than their competitors, held the northern portion for a time, while Holland had to limit herself to the section between New Amsterdam and Albany.

For a short period a fifth power made its appearance—Sweden. As early as 1626 Gustavus Adolphus, the hero of that age, sought a foothold here. He contributed four hundred thousand dollars to the organization of a company of merchants seeking refuge for persecuted Protestants and, of course, mixing a bit of business with it. But Gustavus became involved in the Thirty Years' War in Germany and was killed in the battle of Lützen. Oxenstierna, the great Swedish minister, took up the work, and four years later the enterprise reached fruition.

Peter Minuit quit the services of New Netherland and became the manager of the first Swedish colony in America. The colonists were very much impressed with the place and called Cape Henlopen the Point of Paradise. The entire portion on the west side of the bay and up the river to the falls of Trenton was honorably purchased from the Indians and named New Sweden. The creek and the fort which they built on the spot were named in honor of Christiana, maiden queen of Sweden.

The colony prospered greatly, and immigration was rapid and constant. The people seemed quite happy, and no settlers in America showed more ability or intelligence in the direction of their affairs. From the first, however, the authorities of New Amsterdam looked askance upon the newcomers, whom they considered interlopers. Remonstrances to Queen Christiana did not avail them. On the contrary, the Swedes built an impregnable fort of hemlock logs on the island of Tinicum, about six miles away from the mouth of the Schuylkill, and were ready to defend themselves.

Because of the protracted war between New Netherland and the Indians, the Swedes were left alone. By geographic imperative, however, they were destined to annihilation sooner or later. In September 1655, eighteen years after their first landing, the Swedes were forced to surrender to the Dutch, who themselves were to be defeated ten years later by the English.

The struggle narrowed to the two contestants—the Dutch

and the English. For a time there was armed peace and watchful waiting, and so we shall return to the story of the Empire State as it was acquiring shape and personality.

Van Twiller was still governor, and his eye was centered upon the prosperity of Manhattan. To prove the importance of New Amsterdam, he conferred upon it the "staple right." Vessels carrying merchandise up the River had to stop and pay duties whether they discharged there or not. How shall man know his power unless he uses it to hurt others?

Centuries later, Brooklyn became famous for having "a tree"; at this juncture, it had a ferry, which united it to New Amsterdam for the price of three stivers in "wampum," about six cents. And already there was racial discrimination, for the Indians had to pay double the rate.

There was still the problem of enticing settlers to New Netherland. The Company managed the affairs poorly, because not the people but quick profits were its chief concern, and yet without the people there would be no profits at all. This dilemma forced it again and again to make concessions. Free passage was offered for settlers and their families, and their livestock was well taken care of during the trip, each animal having its attendant. Schooling for children was promised and for spiritual needs *Krankbesoekers* or *Ziekentorsters*—lay readers and consolers of the sick. They could substitute for clergymen, and were, of course, paid less and thus more easily obtainable. And God, being of the family, wouldn't mind a bit of shabbiness, as long as His children prospered and their purses swelled.

At first the conventional farm crops were cultivated. Later, in emulation of the English colonists in Virginia, tobacco was raised. And since Virginia had slaves, why not use them also on the River? Captured or traded for in the West Indies, the Company brought them in, although the settlers did not seem too anxious to have them. Not because of humanitarian impulses. Philosopher, priest, statesman—all found excellent arguments, eloquently expounded, that man has the right to degrade his fellow-man below the wild beast of the forest and the tame one of the field and the yard. They who win fix the scales, proving that the strong are also the just. The conqueror's conscience is always clear.

The settler did not wish the Negroes because they were chiefly in need of mechanics and traders, and the slaves were neither. However, the Company used them on its own *bouweries* or as house servants to officials.

The farm houses were built, piecemeal, room by room, as the needs developed, and while the sum total was a bit queer, it also had a charm of its own, as caprices generally have. There were low walls, tiny windows placed to suit the fancy, or so it seemed, and, as if dictated by swaggering vanity, the roofs were high and sweeping. Generally speaking, the material used was stone. It was both abundant and easy to handle, and could withstand more valiantly the torch and the arrow of the Indian. There were loopholes in the walls, large enough for muskets to show their threatening mouths to the prospective foe. All in all, "The Dutchman's house is like his breeches, capable of holding anything he can cram into them."

The Dutchman loved his gullet and his belly. He ate rugged food and loads of it. Pasture and garden, orchard and dairy, river and forest—all yielded to his vast appetite. There were pies and puddings, pickles and preserves, scrapple and sausage, salt fish and sauerkraut and soused pigs' feet, bird and deer, pumpkins and potatoes and turnips and carrots.

And in the cellar, barrels of cider and ale and jugs of rum and gin and bottles of wine. And where was there better tobacco than in the land of the Indian? But the Indian's copper pipe the Dutchman disdained. His was painted porcelain and had an enormous stem brought from the country beyond and below the sea.

The attire varied according to rank and purse. The patroon wore broadcloth and velvet, a flowing cape (and the more buttons the more patroon), silver buckles on shoes, and hat broad in the brim with a feather waving like a conqueror's flag.

The ladies wore countless petticoats under billowy skirts, and steel-lined corsets. Much easier in those days to be a Caesar dismantling fortresses than a Don Juan dismantling virtue. And they call them the good old days.

The farmer had to content himself with a *hemdrock,* a shirt of cotton or wool, and in the cold weather a *paltrok* of cloth, a steeple-hat, and wooden shoes. There was also a pair of leather shoes in the house for solemn occasions.

The richer burgher brought fine furnishings from the Old World and, surrounded by them, he began to feel at home, creating the atmosphere of "proper stations" in life. As for the patroons, they assumed the airs of lords and ladies of high degree. And if it is true that oppressing the weak and the poor is the sign of nobility, then they were, indeed, lords and ladies of high degree.

Wouter Van Twiller continued in his blundering way until he was supplanted in 1638 by William Kieft. Kieft was a proponent of energy, spiritual ancestor of the tireless go-getter in our business, politics, and the arts. He was conceited, rapacious, and unbending. Without these attributes, he would have been daunted by the state of affairs in New Amsterdam. The Fort, as usual, was in ruins, public structures in dilapidation, only one windmill still danced to the tune of the winds, the Company's farms were thrown into pasturage, and the people were self-willed and cynical.

Manifestoes began to make their appearances in conspicuous places, calling for righteous conduct and a sense of duty on the part of the public. They were reminded that New Amsterdam had already achieved the status of a village and appropriate attitudes were in order. He forbade rebellion, theft, perjury, and calumny; demanded diligence and subordination; confined sailors to their vessels after nightfall; levied fines on soldiers for swearing, speaking scandal of comrades, intoxication, and firing a musket without orders.

Kieft regulated currency, which was in bad shape. Counterfeit was rampant. Because there was so little coin in circulation, however, inferior grades of shell-money were not prohibited lest "the laboreres and boors and other common people having no other money might be great losers."

He encouraged stock-raising and annual fairs and regulated the retailing of liquors. And since Manhattan attracted both permanent visitors and transients, he built at the Company's expense "a fine hotel of stone" called the *Harberg*, or tavern, on the bank of the East River. Three stories in height and fifty feet square, it was the embryonic skyscraper.

There were no streets in New Amsterdam, and whatever there were of thoroughfares had no names, but rather nicknames suggested by the topography or other incidentals. The narrow, crooked streets around Wall Street bear witness alike to the circuitous foot-paths of our ancestors and the circuitous financial paths of our contemporaries.

There were, though, two principal roads—one beginning at the Fort, traversing the shore along Pearl Street and thence along Peck Slip to Brooklyn ferry; and the other along present Broadway to *Maagde Paatje*, "Maiden Lane." They say that it was so called because the Dutch young ladies would come there to wash their clothes in the stream which ran through it. But for that reason they would have called it

"Laundry Lane" or "Washerwoman's Land"; "Maiden Lane"
evokes lovelier images than linen and soap and battledores.

> Down Maiden Lane, where clover grew,
>   Sweet-scented in the early air,
> Where sparkling rills went shining through
>   Their grassy banks, so green and fair,
>
> Blithe little maids from Holland land
>   Went tripping, laughing each to each,
> To bathe the flax, or spread a band
>   Of linen in the sun to bleach.
>
> Two hundred years ago and more
>   Those thrifty damsels, one by one,
> With plump, round arms their linen bore
>   To dry in Mana-ha-ta's sun. . . .

Kieft appointed a surveyor to locate boundaries and bring
some sort of symmetry in alinement. Things seemed to hum
when the Governor took it into his head, perhaps for per-
sonal enrichment or glory, to proclaim that the Indians, particularly those around Manhattan, had to pay a tribute of
corn, furs and "sewant." If they refused, he would institute
ways "to remove their reluctance."

The Indians answered with pride and unassailable logic.

[They] wondered how the sachem at the Fort dared to exact such
things from them. He must be a very shabby fellow; he had come
in their land when they had not invited him, and now he came
to deprive them of their corn for nothing. The soldiers at the
Fort did not protect the Indians when engaged in war with other
tribes. At such a time the Indians crept together like cats upon
a piece of cloth, and could be killed a thousand times before any
tidings could arrive at the Fort. They had allowed the Dutch to
take possession of the country peaceably; they had never de-

manded anything for it, and therefore the Dutch were indebted
to the Indians rather than the Indians to the Dutch. Moreover
the Indians paid full price for everything they bought, and there
was no reason why they should give the Hollanders corn for
nothing. . . . If we have ceded to you the country you are living
in, we yet remain masters of what we have kept for ourselves.

Thus began the shameful war upon the Indians, which
brought so much tragedy on both sides and emphasized the
tyrannical nature of the Governor toward his own people,
whom he fined and banished without appeal to Holland and
who finally rose in rebellion against him.

A popular party, headed by De Vries, defied his authority
and demanded his removal. In 1647 Kieft embarked for
Europe, but the merchantman in which he sailed was dashed
to pieces on the coast of Wales by a storm, and the former
Governor of New Netherland found a watery grave. As he
deserved? How can one tell? How shall we evaluate each
strand of the pattern; against what background place the
pattern itself? The claim that time alone is the perfect judge
is based upon the false premise that when passions cool, truth
emerges. But passions form an integral part of truth, and
time judges the body without the nerves. The hero defeated
is a traitor. They rule best who are not in power.

9 Of Flesh and Wood

"LIKE unto a peacock, with great state and pomp," Petrus Stuyvesant, "Lord General," "Redresser-General" of all grievances, arrived at Manhattan in the month of May, in the year of Our Lord 1647.

The people of New Amsterdam used up nearly all the powder in the fort as salute to the old soldier, former governor of Curaçao, where he had lost a leg attacking the Portuguese.

The dignitaries welcomed him standing and with uncovered heads, while he, hat on, "as if he were the Grand Duke of Muscovy ... had sat down at his ease in order the better to give audience," chronicles an observer. Quite possibly he, like many another contemporary, had believed that Kieft's departure meant a new era of democracy was about to be inaugurated. In truth, however, Stuyvesant was thoroughly incapable of democratic procedures. He was a typical soldier —imperious, resolute, a martinet. Yet he was not intentionally unjust and had a certain affection for the people. "I shall govern you as a father his children for the advantage of the chartered West India Company, and these burghers, and this land." Moreover, he swore "under the blue heaven" equal justice to all.

Stuyvesant's first care was to conciliate the Indians. He was shrewd enough to realize that their animosity was a festering sore which needed immediate ministration. By liberal concessions, and perhaps because of his very frankness and bluntness, he won the red men's confidence and friendship. Indeed, so intimate and cordial became the relations between the Dutch and the Indians that the English suspected them of making common cause against them.

He was not so anxious to gain the friendship and confidence of the Jews.

In the year 1654 the Dutch lost control of Brazil, and the great Jewish community of Recife had to flee for safety from the Holy Office. One barque, *St. Charles,* reached New Amsterdam with twenty-three penniless refugees. Since their goods at the public auction did not bring enough money to pay Jacques de la Motthe, the captain, for his trouble at having saved from the stake his fellow human beings, they were placed under civil arrest.

Peter Stuyvesant was for immediate expulsion. He would not have in his colony the "hateful enemies and blasphemers of the name of Christ," and wrote to the Directors of the Dutch West India Company in Amsterdam asking for confirmation that "none of the Jewish nation be permitted to infest New Netherland."

The reply was:

We would have liked to agree to your wishes and request, that the new territories should not be further invaded by people of the Jewish race, for we foresee from such immigration the same difficulties which you fear [but] it would be unreasonable and unfair, especially because of the considerable loss sustained by the Jews in the taking of Brazil, and also because of the large amount of capital which they have invested in the shares of this Company.

Blood and money extracted from the Lord General a begrudged haven, but he forbade them to trade to Fort Orange

(Albany) and the South River (Delaware); he forbade also
the purchase of real estate. They were not to be employed in
any public service nor allowed to open retail shops. On the
other hand, to defray the cost of erecting the outer fence of
the town from which Wall Street takes its name, the Jews
had imposed upon them the tax of a thousand florins, equal
to that imposed on the wealthiest only.

Even the request for a burial ground was at first denied
the Jews on the basis that "there was no need for it yet." A
year later there was need, and a lot was granted them outside of the city limits.

And in this fashion, the Lord General was as a father to
his children, and there was "equal justice to all."

Nevertheless, Stuyvesant towered over his predecessors,
and the period of the Dutch control falls quite naturally into
two major divisions: Pre-Stuyvesant and Stuyvesant. The
twenty-one years of occupation and the six governors who
preceded him would have hardly achieved anything of historical proportions without the climax of seventeen years of
Stuyvesant's reign. Moreover, despite the angry stamping of
his wooden leg carved and encrusted with gold, despite his
fog-horn of a voice thundering commands and "ill words
which would better suit the fish market"; despite that "whoever had him opposed had as much as the sun and moon
against him," it was under him that the first distinctly municipal form of government came into being in New Amsterdam
on February 2, 1653. It resembled our present-day body of
aldermen. He also proclaimed a bench of justices.

However limited in authority both of these bodies really
were, they fed the desire for greater and still greater share
in government affairs and laid the foundation of a democratic society.

Before long citizenship rights were demanded and were

granted by law on February 2, 1657. The great burgher-right conferred citizenship on all officials, burgomasters, clergymen, and commissioned officers of the city regiment. The small-burgher right was conferred upon all male inhabitants "who had kept fire and light within the City one year and six weeks," to all native-born, and to those who married native-born daughters of the burghers.

Meanwhile, all along the banks of the Hudson, there was activity—trading, farming, building—building homes, building boats, building towns. The River was alive with boats— mast vessels, barks, sloops, canoes—stopping at all the "reaches" between Manhattan and Albany. The first "reach" extended past the long wall of the Palisades, the second included the Tappan Zee and took the voyager up to Haverstraw, which was the third. Beyond Haverstraw was Seylmaker's Reach, then Hoge's, followed by Vorsen's which included the dangerous passage of the Highlands. Then came Fisher's Reach, Playsier, Vaste, Hunter, until Kinderhook was reached.

Toward the end of the Dutch regime the city of New Amsterdam had as many as fifty ships, twenty sloops, and thirty boats, nor did this indicate by any means the size of the River trade or the size of the fleet at its wharves. Solid vessels, many of these, and mighty sailors to man them. Sometimes "the white wings" would travel in flocks of six or more, like great seagulls, glowing in the sun, while the cliffs crowned with forests forever seemed to threaten them with impending doom and eagles screamed their challenge or their warning.

It took days—a week or more—to make the trip from one end of the River to the other. But this was not their only destination. These boats cut across the River, plunged into seas and oceans—to Europe, to the West Indies, to the Orient, and put out with whatever Neptune blew.

So adventurous were those old skippers at times that they had to be restrained by orders of the Amsterdam Court, and even the voyagers had to have passes, "for such is found necessary for the better security of this City. Done at Fort Willem Hendrick."

There was activity also across the River from Manhattan, the district now known as New Jersey. No building of boats, to be sure, but farms and homes; and Jersey City itself, originally known as Paulus, Powles, or Pauws Hook, served as one of the chief means of communication between the two shores.

Then there was Hobock, an Indian village, later known as Hoboquin and finally as Hoboken. It made its bow in history with murders and massacres, arson and pillage. Who was guilty? Who started it—the Indians or the whites? We shall never be able to disentangle the multitudinous threads of events. It is easy to say that it takes two to make a quarrel, or that in human disasters one may assume that there is a fifty-fifty responsibility. We must never forget, however, that the whites were the intruders, that the whites proclaimed from thousands of pulpits the brotherhood of man, that the whites were the stronger, that the whites claimed a Christian civilization which implied charity and love and understanding and patience.

At any rate, the Dutch crossed the River at night and massacred a hundred men, women, and children on Castle Point, one of the promontories. Did Domine Bogardus thunder against the murderers? Did he call it a black spot on Christendom in general and New Netherland in particular? There is no record of contrition or penance. The blood mingled with the waters of the River, and the River flowed on. The flesh was devoured by eagle and jackal, and the bones crumbled into dust. Upon the Tree of Time each generation carves its hoop of misery and shame.

The west shore of the River provided many gruesome tales. There is the one about the *Guests from Gibbet Island,* a roistering and swaggering crew which caused a pandemonium at the inn of the "Wild Goose" and shocked the respectable burgers of Cummunipaw beyond measure. Eventually, however:

At a table on which burnt a light as blue as brimstone, sat the three guests from Gibbet Island with halters around their necks and, bobbing their ghostly cups together, trolled the old Dutch freebooter's glee:

> For three merry lads be we;
> And three merry lads be we;
> I on the land, and thou on the sand,
> And Jack on the gallows tree.

At the Elysian Fields, near Weehawken, there was a grotto called the Sybyl's Cave which contained a spring of clear water much sought after. There the beautiful maiden, Mary Rogers, disappeared. Was it murder? Was it elopement? How much truth? How much legend? Edgar Allan Poe based his *Mystery of Marie Roget* upon it: however, he changed the girl's nationality and moved the scene from the Hudson to the Seine, those being the days when the Left Bank of Paris pullulated with romance and tragedy, triumph and despair.

And how populated were the forests and the hills and the caves with spirits and gnomes and ghosts and witches and hobgoblins and demons and creatures for which good Christians had no names. What did they do there? Why had they all gathered from hell and hunting ground, from grave and pit? Is man's mind a vast swamp where Illusion spawns? Is reality illusion or illusion reality?

Meanwhile, Stuyvesant was forever "busy building, laying masonry, making, breaking, repairing and the like; but generally in matters of the Company," without, however, neglecting himself. "The Governor is everything, and does the business of the whole country, having several shops himself. . He is a brewer, is a part owner of ships, a merchant and a trader."

While he ordered the fences fixed internally, Stuyvesant saw to his fences externally. In 1650 the Governor met the ambassadors of the Eastern colonies at Hartford and, after much palaver which hid much bad faith, a boundary line was fixed between New England and New Netherland. The line established extended across Long Island north and south, passing through Oyster Bay, and thence to Greenwich, on the other side of the sound. From this point north the dividing line was practically identical with the present boundary of Connecticut on the west. The treaty was ratified by the colonies, by the West India Company, and by the States-General of Holland. The English government, having other plans, treated the whole matter with contemptuous indifference.

10 Pâté de Foie Gras

PIETER STUYVESANT'S governorship had now lasted for seven years—years neither quite lean nor quite fat—but the Company evidently considered him sufficiently able and persuasive to order him to take a trip to the West Indies and stir up business there for a while.

The burgomasters and the *schepens* (aldermen) tendered him a "gay repast" at the city hall. In turn Stuyvesant, on behalf of the Dutch West India Company, presented to Martin Krieger, the presiding burgomaster, the seal of New Amsterdam, something for which they had yearned for a long time.

The seal had an "argent per pale, with three crosses saltire; for a crest a beaver topper surmounted by a mantle on which was a shield argent bearing the letters G. W. C. (*Geoctrouiuyeerde West-Indische Compagnie*—Chartered West India Company)." Under the base of the arms were the words: "*Sigillum Amstello Damensis in Novo Belgio*"— the whole surrounded by a wreath of laurels.

Upon his return, while liquidating the Swedish colony, he found himself unexpectedly in trouble with the Indians, due to the shooting of a squaw by a former *schout fiscal*, or public prosecutor and sheriff, for stealing peaches in his orchard. A company of nearly two thousand Indians wreaked vengeance by slaughtering and pillaging. Once again Stuyvesant, however, succeeded in pacifying the Indians without resort to war, and it gave him the opportunity to warn the people that the defenses were in bad shape and that the fortifications were inadequate. The response was weak, and the time was not far away for the pay-off.

While the quarrels between the burghers of New Amsterdam with their rulers went on, sometimes acrimoniously, sometimes drearily, the patroonships continued to grow and prosper, as did the evils thereof.

The most famous—or infamous—of the patroons was a man by the name of Kiliaen Van Rensselaer. He had been a prosperous jeweler of Amsterdam and applied for a patroonship on the Hudson in 1629. With the help of a Comforter of the Sick—subdoctor, subpastor, who performed operations, marriages, funeral services, and similar fateful functions—Van Rensselaer robbed the colony and despoiled the tenants, while his descendants continued for generations the malodorous practices.

Van Rensselaer was an absentee landlord. He never set foot on his great Hudson River patroonship, which by constant machinations finally swelled to the proportion of an entire state. He would not endure the rigors of a new world. Why should he, if he could fill his diamond-studded bags with florins made by the sweat and blood of his workers and tenants, who later numbered several thousand?

Setting up a commissary to sell supplies to his tenants at exorbitant prices, he wrote to the governor of New Netherland, confidentially: "I would not like my people to get too wise and figure out their master's profit, especially in matters in which they themselves are interested . . . these I would rather keep a secret between the Company and myself. . . ."

But even if the tenants had had all the data, they would have found it quite impossible to do the figuring properly, for public education in the patroonship was limited to two

R's only—'rithmetic being reserved solely for the sons of the bosses. Since religion was particularly emphasized in the miserable schools, however, the tenants could wait in patience until they reached the Great Patroonship in the Valley of Heaven to count their treasures. The ancient tyrants feared the education of the masses; the modern ones are shrewder—they fear the lack of education. An illiterate man might think for himself, stammeringly and in monosyllables to be sure, but he remains unpredictable; the man appropriately "educated" is securely glued and nailed within the required frame.

Nor did Johannes Van Rensselaer, son of Kiliaen, deign to cross the ocean to take a look at the good River and the kind Valley, magical horns of plenty, forever replenishing and then emptying themselves into the deep coffers of the family.

The people of Rensselaerswyck had to wait for three generations before they were honored with the permanent presence of their lord. The fourth generation, in the shape of Stephen, built the Van Rensselaer manor house, the most palatial home in the New World.

Like some European kingly dynasty, the Rensselaers married and became allied to the other wealthy patroons—the Van Cortlandts, the Schuylers, the Livingstons, the Nicollses, the Wattses. Never did the Assembly lack a representative of some branch of these families. When it was bruited about that a patroon would come into New York by land, crowds would turn out to see him drive through Broadway in coach and four—a royal prince.

No chains are harder to break than the golden ones of the benevolent tyrant, the big "father," and until the middle of the nineteenth century the feudal system instituted by the jeweler of Amsterdam plagued the farmers of the Hudson Valley, forcing them more than once to armed rebellion.

Quite possibly there would have been no "embattled farm-

ers" revolting against the tyranny of the British if they had
not hoped that their sacrifices would bring an end to their
local tyranny as well. The British were defeated, but not the
patroons. The ancient yoke still pressed, while the cynical
philosophy of the masters resolved itself in the maxim that
no ladder of success rises quite as high as that whose rungs
are the necks of people.

Whatever sacrifices the wealthy River families made for
national independence, they were ready neither to relinquish
their grip on their lands nor to lighten the burdens of those
who had worked upon them for generations. On the contrary,
they increased their holdings by adding to them the properties confiscated from the Tories, and while preaching democracy and the equality of all men they practiced all the evils
of the aristocracy of the Old World, whose replantation had
been so successful in the New One.

Three important units were finally established—Fort Amsterdam, Fort Orange, and Rensselaerswyck. The West India
Company had, however, complete political and trade sovereignty over them. It enacted laws, administered justice, and
appointed governors and other officials.

"Old Silver Nails," as Stuyvesant was nicknamed, continued his reign of stamping his wooden leg, flying into rages,
and thundering, and yet doing his duty according to his
lights.

The population of New Netherland continued to spread in
various directions. Long Island had already been purchased
from the Canarsies, and Coney Island (from the Indian of
Conynge—"Rabbit") acquired for the price of a pound of
shot. Religious persecution in the English colonies had driven
many settlers into the present Queens Borough and Westchester County, and to the glory of the Dutch let it be said
that not one witch was ever burned on their soil. The Ann

Hutchinson family had already settled in the region of New Rochelle; the Pell family had given their name to Pelham; Thomas Stiles and his associates incorporated the town of Flushing.

New Amsterdam, too, broadened its flanks. Dr. de la Montagne formed the germ of modern Yorkville. James Bronck gave his name to the Bronx Borough. Jan Evertsen Bout and a few others settled in *Breuckelen,* "broken ground," now Brooklyn. In 1658, the Governor offered a ferry to Long Island and a clergyman to any twenty-five families that would plant a village in northern Manhattan, and so New Harlem was born, in memory of Haarlem in Holland.

The latter years of Stuyvesant's regime were peaceful and gay, and prosperity was general. Eighteen languages could be heard on the sidewalks of New Amsterdam, and an official interpreter had to be appointed. Many of the citizens were traders who brought back rich prizes from many parts of the world, and the commercial foundation of the Metropolis was firmly laid.

Despite all this, it was evident that the Dutch rule in what was to become the Empire State was a failure. The inhabitants of New Netherland blamed it on the selfish greed of the Company and the unconcern of the mother country. But it was not wholly so, for the people themselves were interested chiefly in mulcting the Indian, robbing him of his furs for valueless trinkets and poisonous liquor, while the officials filled their bottomless purses and planned to return home some day in grand style.

There were also their neighbors, north and south and west, who tantalized their envy. Boston had outgrown New Amsterdam. The schools of Massachusetts and Connecticut flourished whereas the academy in Manhattan had had only a sickly career of two years. Virginia was prospering. There

were heavy taxes levied in New Netherland to support the
poor; New England claimed she had no poor. Liberty and
rights were hotly debated in the English villages; the Dutch
farmers and traders either dared not indulge in these luxuries
or would not.

The morale of the inhabitants of New Netherland crumbled, and they were soon to demonstrate that they were
ready to betray their mother country and accept the new
rulers. Meanwhile they refused to obey laws or pay taxes,
and the severe penalties inflicted in the name of God and
King—branding, lashing, mutilation, the rack, and the gibbet
—only infuriated them more. And the rulers would soon reap
the evil weeds which flourish in the backyard of injustice.

1664. England and Holland were at peace, and the treaty
of 1650 fixed the boundary lines between the Dutch and the
English possessions. There was also the treaty of 1654, con-
tracted between Cromwell, the Lord Protector, and the High
Mightinesses. So what was there to worry about? There was
indeed a great deal to worry about, for the year 1663 had
been an evil one for the people of New Netherland. Flood
had destroyed the crops; an epidemic of smallpox had broken
out; earthquake had shaken the houses; and there were always the Indians. And Stuyvesant was still thundering about
the streets which needed pavements and the fortress which
needed mortar and the lack of discipline.

In 1660 the Restoration replaced Charles II on the English
throne. And promptly he reinterpreted the treaty of his Puritan Predecessor by reviving the old Navigation Act, which
made it necessary for all English commerce to be carried on
in English ships exclusively. But there was New Amsterdam
holding the key position on the Eastern coast and doing a
lively trade with New England under another flag. That
must cease. The Eastern coast belonged to England. New

Amsterdam belonged to England. New Netherland belonged to England. By what right? John Cabot discovered the continent. Not the continent, precisely, but he skirted Labrador, didn't he? And Sebastian Cabot, his son, may have touched the Hudson Bay. And Hudson was an Englishman, wasn't he? An Englishman is always an Englishman. The Cabots were Italians? They were made admirals in the British navy, weren't they? And so, the whole continent belonged to England. There was also the question of the strength of the navy, which must not be neglected. God always helps him who helps himself, and England has always been a God-abiding nation.

1664. And His Majesty granted his brother James, Duke of York and Albany, a patent of Long Island and of the mainland between the Connecticut and the Delaware, including, quite simply, the whole of the Dutch possessions in America.

The Duke of York despatched four ships and five hundred veteran troops under the command of Colonel Richard Nicolls, named governor of the province not yet his. In July the armament reached Boston and thence proceeded against New Amsterdam. On the 28th of August the fleet passed the Narrows and anchored at Gravesend Bay, and before the Dutch had recovered from the surprise, Long Island was subdued.

Pretending not to know the meaning of the errand of the fleet, Stuyvesant sent a commission of four to inquire. In response, the English sent four of their own demanding the surrender "of the town situated on the island commonly known by the name of Manhattoes." To which they added a proclamation assuring protection of person and property to all who submitted voluntarily.

Stuyvesant sent to Nicolls a lengthy statement about the Dutch rights. It would have been much more effective if he also could have pointed to a fortress which did not so easily succumb to the snout of a hog in search of refuse; if he had had more than a few hundred pounds of powder and a mere dozen guns with one hundred and fifty regular soldiers to man them; if the burghers had had a will to fight; if the magistrates and the clergymen had not joined the women and children in imploring submission. "Of what avail," pleaded Domine Megapolensis, "are our poor guns against that broadside of more than sixty? It is wrong to shed blood to no purpose."

Therefore the answer of Colonel Nicolls was precisely the answer strength offers weakness that "they were not come here to dispute about it, but to execute their order and commission without fail either peacefully or by force; and if they had anything to dispute about it, it must be done with His Majesty of England, as they could do nothing here in the premises."

There was another bit of palaver between "Old Silver Nails" and the Englishman, something about "tomorrow."

"Tomorrow, I will speak with you in Manhattan," said the Colonel.

"Friends will be welcome if they come in a friendly manner," said the Governor.

"I shall come with my ships and soldiers, and he will be a bold messenger indeed who shall then dare to come on board and solicit terms. Raise the white flag of peace at the fort, and then something may be considered."

"Well, let it be so; I would much rather be carried to my grave."

But had he really desired to be a hero, he should have committed suicide on the spot, for heroes must die at the appropriate moment. Instead, two days after the official surrender, the Dutch garrison, with ex-Governor Petrus Stuyvesant at the head, marched out "with their arms, drums beating, and colors flying and lighted matches."

The fort was renamed Fort James; New Amsterdam became New York, as well as the province. All public rights and franchises of the Dutch West India Company were henceforth vested in the Duke of York. Governor Nicolls was very much pleased with the town and wrote to the Duke that it was "the best of all His Majesty's towns in America."

There was general good will. The burgomasters and *schepens* wrote to the Dutch West India Company that: "Since we have no longer to depend on your Honor's promises of protection, we . . . must fly for refuge to the Almighty . . . not doubting but He will stand by us in this sorely afflicting conjuncture."

To the Duke of York, they wrote: "It has pleased God to bring us under your Royal Highness' obedience wherein we promise to conduct ourselves as good subjects are bound to do." As to the Honorable Colonel Nicolls, they were "confident and assured that under the wings of this valiant gentleman we shall bloom and grow like the cedar on Lebanon."

To Heer Stuyvesant the burgomasters and *schepens* gave a certificate of comportment to take to Holland where he would have to defend his conduct before the Company and the government.

We, the undersigned schout, burgomasters and schepens of the city of New Yorck on the island of Manathan, formerly named New Amsterdam, certify and declare, at the request of the Honorable Petrus Stuyvesant, late Director General of New Netherland, and who now on the change by the English is about to return to Patria, that his Honor has during about eighteen years administration conducted and demeaned himself not only as a Director General according to the best of our knowledge ought to do, on all occurring circumstances, for the interest of the West

India Company, but besides as an honest proprietor and patriot of this province and a supporter of the reformed religion.

It helped greatly. Stuyvesant was completely vindicated, returned to Manhattan, gave up his house on Whitehall Street to the new governor for an official residence, and retired to his *bouwerie.*

It was a well-tended *bouwerie,* stocked with the finest in horses, cattle, and sheep and occupying the space now bounded by Sixth and Seventh Streets, and by Fourth Avenue and the East River. His roomy wooden house was girt about by orchards and flower gardens, and a pear tree which he brought from Holland remained one of the landmarks of the town until it was blown down two centuries later during the great snowstorm of February 1867. Its wood was cut up into mementoes and was treasured in many city homes.

Stuyvesant lived on for eight happy and peaceful years and at the age of eighty passed on to his reward. He was buried beneath the chapel built by himself on his farm. His widow survived him for ten years and her will founded St. Mark's Church—"St. Marks-in-the-Bouwerie"; the present edifice, erected in 1802, stands upon the site.

A tablet is built in the outer eastern wall with the following inscription:

In this vault lies buried
PETRUS STUYVESANT
Late Captain General and Governor-in-Chief of Amsterdam
in New Netherland, and now called New York,
And the Dutch West India Islands, died in A. D. 1672
aged 80 Years.

And so the "goose with the fat points" after sixty years became *pâté de foie gras* for the English, and the flag of the

Kingdom of the Netherlands which Captain Henry Hudson had planted in the Valley of De Groote River was lowered. Not quite for all time, for once again in 1673 the Dutch arrived with a fleet of twenty-three boats and sixteen hundred men under the command of Evertsen and Binckes, and now it was the turn of the English commissioners to demand why they had come "in such hostile manner to disturb his majesty's subjects in this place." And since the English were not prepared to fight, the admirals retorted simply that they came to take what was "their own and their own they would have." And they did, but it only lasted for one year, during which the new masters distinguished themselves by tyrannical ordinances, among them one dedicated to the strict observance of the Sabbath. It prohibited

from sunrise to sundown . . . all sorts of handicraft, trade and traffic, gaming, boat racing, or running with carts or wagons, fishing, fowling, running and picking nuts, strawberries and the like, all riotous racing, calling and shouting of children in the streets, together with all unlawful exercises and games, drunkenness, frequenting taverns or tap-houses, dancing, card-playing, rolling ninepins or bowls . . . which is more in vogue on this than on any other day.

And when "on the tenth of November, anno 1674, the province of New Netherland" was, according to the treaty of peace concluded between England and Netherlands, surrendered "by Governor Colve to Governor Major Edmund Andros in behalf of his majesty of Great Britain," there were no tears shed and no certificates of comportment issued.

Now the supremacy of Great Britain in America was established, and from northern Maine to southern Georgia the American coast was under the flag of England.

11 New Masters—Old Evils

F IRST came the names. "And out of the ground the Lord
God formed every beast of the field and every fowl of
the air; and brought them unto Adam to see what he would
call them: and whatsoever Adam called every living creature,
that was the name thereof."

And the name of New Netherland and New Amsterdam
henceforth was New York, and that of Beverwyck was Albany, in honor of James Stuart, Duke of Albany and York,
into whose lap dropped from the palsied hands of the Dutch
the vast estate. But if places were named for people because
of merit or service, certainly neither the great Metropolis nor
the capital of the Empire State should have their present
appellations. James Stuart was narrow-minded, vicious, and
greedy and had not the least conception of the historic significance of the country which had become his by royal fiat.

Richard Nicolls, the first governor, however, was a better
man than his master, and all in all his short rule of three
years proved beneficial. His first big job was that of deter-
mining the limits of the boundaries of the Duke's possessions.
It was troublesome and vexatious. Then there was the matter of weights, measures, and coins, and above all the introduction of the new language. No easy task for the *Heeren*
and *Vrouwen,* proud of their own tongue, and so rhetorical,
to be constrained to stammer sounds which somehow resem-

bled theirs and yet were so different and really so ridiculous. Besides, all commercial documents as well as all official intercourse were required to be in English.

"Now it seems it has pleased the Lord to ordain that we must learn English," wrote Van Rensselaer to his mother. "The worst of it all is that we already for nearly four years have been under this jurisdiction and that as yet I have learned so little. The reason is that no one has any liking for it."

And a century later, in one of the frank memoirs of the day, one reads that at last "the English language began to be more generally understood."

The "patroonship" was changed to the "manor" and *Mijnheer* to "Lord," but whatever the new regulations and laws, the tenant was still at the mercy of the one who owned the land.

The Dutch continued to come to their lost colony and often intermarried with the English. The population increased. The Indians, decimated, became less and less of a menace.

But Nicolls returned to England to take care of his own affairs and some years later died a soldier's death on the battlefield. His successor, Colonel Francis Lovelace, was less capable, more tyrannical, and rather obtuse in psychology. He was enraged to find that the people of New York had the "breeding of courts," resenting fiercely being treated as inferiors by the British.

It was ever the custom of the British to treat "natives" with hauteur. Chosen to colonial posts by virtue of nepotism, unscrupulousness, and general ignorance, governors and their staffs strutted like vicious peacocks, without the grace of plumes. Jealous of their prerogatives as well as of the culture of those who had the misfortune of being under them (a culture which they could only guess at, but were incapable of understanding), they always brought not only misery of body but anguish of mind.

Lovelace, spurred by the Duke, piled taxes upon taxes upon the inhabitants. Protests against the government and petitions for redress were rejected with contempt. "If there is any more murmuring against the taxes, make them so heavy that the people can do nothing but think how to pay them," was the Governor's cynical order.

Nevertheless, under pressure of circumstances Lovelace issued orders which helped the growth and betterment of the conditions of the city and the state, chief among them being the establishment of a regular monthly mail service between New York and Boston.

I here present you, [the Governor of New York wrote to Governor Winthrop] with two rarities, a packet of the latest intelligence I could meet withal, and a post . . . so that if it receive but the same ardent inclinations from you as at first it hath from myself, by our monthly advisos all public occurrences may be transmitted between us . . . consonant to the commands laid upon us by His Sacred Majesty, who strictly enjoins all his American subjects to enter into a close correspondency with each other. . . . This person that has undertaken the employment I conceived most proper, being both active, stout and indefatigable. He is sworn as to his fidelity. . . . Hartford is the first stage I have designed him to change his horse, where constantly I expect he should have a fresh one lie. All the letters outward shall be delivered gratis . . . and reciprocally, we expect all to us free. Each first Monday of the month he sets out from New York, and is to return within the month from Boston to us again. . . . Thus you see the scheme I have drawn to promote a happy correspondence. . . . It would be much advantageous to our design, if in the interval you discoursed with some of the most able woodmen, to make out the best and most facile way for a post, which in the process of time would be the king's best highway; as likewise passages and accommodation at rivers, fords, or other necessary places.

And so, the first mail from New York to Boston, which was also the first on the American continent, started on New Year's day, 1673.

The early settlers used their legs and the Indian trails for means of communication. Then followed the horse and the donkey and the wagon and the buggy and, the old roads becoming inadequate, more and wider roads were built. The State accomplished this chiefly from the proceeds of lotteries. The Puritans were not too finicky about games; nor, according to the latest information were they as finicky as represented in the matter of love and its allied branches.

But "The-stream-that-flows-both-ways," now definitely the Hudson River, still held the primal position in the colony. At its head in Albany, it brought the white man into contact with the Indian of the hinterland and gradually with the white man who pushed westward. At its foot, it made contact with the outside world.

Piracy flourished from one end of the River to the other, and pirate captains, upon occasions, were treated as magnificos by the authorities, riding in the governor's "coach and six" through the city. But, then, the daggers which hung from their girdles blazed with jewels. Ah, the honor to be stabbed with such a knife!

The most famous of the pirates was a sea captain, highly respected and prosperous, who was given a boat with thirty-six guns by the authorities to hunt and destroy pirates. And so Captain Kidd set out on his virtuous mission on the good ship *Adventure,* but before long turned pirate himself, the most redoubtable of all.

Captain Kidd was finally hanged and became a legend,

the highest tribute time may pay to timelessness. Had he remained a peaceful citizen he would have died of asthma or the "crab," as cancer was called in those days, and in some beweeded cemetery there might still totter, like an old man's tooth, a stone on which is faintly seen: "Here lieth William Kidd—aetat—[erased]—beloved husband of—[erased]—followed the sea—died in bed—Goodness is rewarded ever, Passer-by forget it never!"

The turnpike was the most interesting of the later means of transportation in the States. The Albany-Schenectady Turnpike, the most famous of them, was completed in 1805 at a cost of ten thousand dollars a mile. Altogether, by 1821, the system included about four thousand miles of improved roads.

What a sight the turnpike presented—stagecoaches and covered wagons; eight-horse teams hauling great loads and slender buggies filled with the more delicate goods; drovers of cattle and pigs; emigrants from many countries carrying bulging valises, their worldly goods tightly gripped in their hands, or slung over their shoulders.

While there were no de luxe hotels on the way, there were many taverns—indeed, on the average one tavern every mile of the road between Albany and Cherry Valley. The guests did not observe the present day convention of impersonality but struck friendships readily, got drunk together, and engaged in mighty brawls.

There were, as a matter of fact, taverns catering exclusively to one class of people or another, thus promising their clientele greater peace and security, or at least fights among peers.

For thirty years the turnpike era continued, but did not prosper. The maintenance costs took most of the profits, and

the dividends no longer attracted shareholders. Eventually
the roads were turned over to the State.

Meanwhile, conditions were shifting. The Dutch had come
once more and left, and Lovelace who had gone to England,
never returned to assume the governorship again. He was
supplanted by Edmund Andros, a young and dashing major
of dragoons. To his credit it may be said that he introduced
a number of civic improvements. He compelled the tanners
to move beyond the city limits and thus purify the air; he
sank a number of wells; built a dock and market-house;
obliged every householder to set his litter and refuse in barrels for the city's carts to carry away; ordered the limitation
of drinks to Indians.

In matters of politics, however, he proved himself even
worse than his predecessor. Arbitrary rule was openly
avowed. Taxes were levied without authority of law, and all
appeals and protestations were treated with derision and
contempt. In 1681 Andros was recalled, and his place taken
by Colonel Thomas Dongan, a Catholic, the King being
Catholic himself.

Dongan had charm and personality and, forced by the
clamor of the people, framed a Charter of Liberties ordain-
ing that:

Supreme legislative power should forever reside in the governor,
council and people, met in general assembly; that every free-
holder and freeman might vote for representatives without re-
strain; that no freeman should suffer but by judgment of his peers,
and that all trials should be by a jury of twelve men; that no tax
should be assessed on any pretence whatever, but by the consent
of assembly; that no seaman or soldier should be quartered on
the inhabitants against their will; that no martial law should exist;
and that no person professing faith in God, by Jesus Christ,

should at any time be in any way disquited or questioned for any
difference of opinion in matters of religion.

Except for the fact that non-Christians were expressly eliminated in the last clause, the document was a laudable one.
Of course it was never meant to be put into practice or long
kept there. It was sent for approval to the Duke and his sig-
nature awaited. But on February 6, 1685, King Charles, making merry among foppish courtiers, had a heart attack and
died. The Duke became James II and at once abrogated the
legislature in New York, levied taxes by arbitrary degrees,
forbade printing presses, and made himself absolute master
of his colonies. In the spring of 1688 New England, New
York, and New Jersey were thrown into one province, and
one governor, none other than Major Andros again, ruled
them all. The major had in the meantime been knighted and
made Sir Edmund.

But the plans of mice and kings "gang aft agley," and
before the year was out, William of Orange landed in Devon-
shire and prepared for battle. In the Spring the last of the
Stuarts became a king-in-exile, the proud governor of all his
majesty's colonies found refuge in a Boston jail, and the reign
of William and Mary was acclaimed by the people at home
and across the ocean.

There was rejoicing in New York, but it was followed by
much trouble and by the hanging of the first rebel against
the tyranny of England.

James II was a Roman Catholic and, had he remained in
power, it had been his resolve to force his faith upon the inhabitants of the New World, composed of ardent Protestants
in mortal fear of the revival of "Papism." His exile did not
completely allay these fears. He had as his friend, Louis XIV
of France, another zealous propagandist of Romanism, who

found it propitious to declare war on England and Holland, with a view of becoming, among other things, master of the New World, which was growing so profitable to royalty squandering the wealth of its people in mad extravagances.

The French with their Indian allies, under Count de Frontenac, were advancing from Canada; they reached Schenectady, left it in ruins, and moved toward Albany. Nicholson, lieutenant-governor, was not the man to cope with the crisis, and many townsfolk suspected him to be a "Papist" in disguise.

Jacob Leisler, a German (married to a Dutch woman), a leading merchant, refused to pay duty on a cargo of wine arrived from Europe on the basis that the flight of James had removed all authorized government in New York. He had been for thirty years a resident of the city, a deacon of the Dutch church, and an implacable enemy of the Roman Church. The refusal to pay duty was, in a sense, the straw that broke the camel's back. The citizens had long been enraged against arbitrary taxation, and now applauded the man who dared to challenge the authorities.

Leisler became the leader of the "popular party," the small shopkeepers, the artisans, the sailors. The Committee of Safety, drawn from the people, appointed him commander-in-chief of the province, and he took possession of the fort. In the spring of 1690 Leisler summoned the first "congress" of the northern colonies and received their confirmation as temporary lieutenant-governor.

Nicholson, meanwhile, leader of the "aristocratic party," the manor lords and the officeholders, left for England. At court he persuaded the king that Leisler was a traitor and a usurper of power, while a royal audience was denied Leisler's friend, Joost Stoll, whom he sent to England to render a full account of the affair.

With that empty, grandiose gesture of spurious justice which lets sheep and wolf fight it out on equal terms in the arena, the king instructed the new governor, Colonel Henry Sloughter, to examine strictly and impartially "into the state of affairs in New York, and to render a true and faithful account thereof."

Of all people—Sloughter, the mercenary and impoverished adventurer, who could be counted upon to become the amenable tool of the "aristocrats"!

Sloughter took no chances. He sailed from England with several ships and a goodly number of soldiers. Leisler was constrained to surrender the fort and stand trial before a jury of foes. What was expected came to pass. Leisler was condemned to hang—he and his assistant, Milborne. Gallows were raised on Leisler's own grounds on the site of the World Building in Park Row.

A crowd composed of weeping friends and gloating enemies assembled on a chilly May morning to witness the performance. The two men accepted their fate with dignity and courage.

So far from revenge do we depart this world [Leisler said] that we require and make it our dying request to all our relations and friends that they should in time to come be forgetful of any injury done to us, or either of us, so that on both sides of the discord and dissension (which were created by the devil in the beginning) may with our ashes be buried in oblivion, never more to rise up for the trouble of posterity.

The drop fell, and so perished the first governor who drew his power from the people themselves. However, the ashes were not buried in oblivion. There were embers within them which in time burst into flames. For years the city was a seething cauldron. Many were the races which jostled one another in the corkscrew streets of the future Gotham, fighting in miniature battles the battles their mother nations fought in grand style in Europe, on the high seas, and on the new continent itself. And even when the roots had been largely destroyed, and the new generations had forgotten the languages and customs and enmities of their ancestors, they still could not stand on the sidelines when the "mother" nations were at one another's throats.

Sloughter died suddenly, a few months after Leisler's execution—poisoned, some said, divine retribution, said others. Fletcher, an Episcopalian, succeeded him, and under his encouragement Trinity Church was raised where it now stands—on a corner of the Old West India Company's *bouwerie*.

Colonel (somehow, throughout the ages it was the "colonel" who oppressed most) Benjamin Fletcher succeeded him. He was a brave and capable soldier, and for that very reason, perhaps, a reprehensible civil administrator. They who draw the sword, before they die by the sword, rule by it. He became the leader of the Aristocrats and tried to enslave the inhabitants by dividing the soil of the province among a few rich families and the Church of England and thus build great tenant-farmed estates.

The Leislerians, remembering their martyr, protested so vigorously that the king was forced to recall the colonel, and sent the Earl of Bellomont in his stead—an honest man, at last, who undid as well as he could the evil of his predecessor, and who showed a penchant for liberty and political equality. He took into his council several leaders of the Leislerian party, and indeed, they became the ruling influence in all the branches of the government. Naturally, he was hated by the rich and the clergy, who rejoiced at his sudden death in 1701. The common people, however, were sorrow-stricken.

Meanwhile, the State and the City of New York prospered. England discouraged manufacturing, but the ocean industries brought wealth, even though a goodly part of it was due to privateering and piracy. Houses sprang up like mushrooms and coffee-houses lent a social atmosphere to the ever increasing population. White and gilded coaches rattled on the cobblestones of the tree-lined streets, but their doors, emblazoned with coats of arms, were opened by Negro slaves.

In the beginning of the eighteenth century class distinction was paramount. At the top swaggered the aristocrats, the lords of the lands and all therein; in the middle hardly anyone, for everybody tried to climb the ladder to the top, but the ladder was slippery and most of them fell back to the bottom where toiled the workers and schemed the small business people. And below these a small group of indentured white servants, some former convicts, some kidnapped and sold into servitude. And lower still, the Negro slaves, grown much more numerous during the English regime, particularly in towns. In the year 1736 the white population in New York City was 11,723; the black 2444—one slave to four freemen.

In Albany the slaves were generally treated kindly, and there is little trouble recorded. In New York, the masters seemed to fear the Negroes, which resulted in ill treatment. There were several ordinances against the Negroes. They might not congregate beyond the number of four; they might not go armed with gun, club, sword, or stone under the penalty of ten lashes at the whipping post; they might not go about the streets at night without lighted lanterns.

And the pay-off—insurrections. In 1712 nine whites were killed and many wounded, for which six Negroes committed suicide, twenty-one were put to death (one was broken on the wheel, a few were burned at the stake, and the rest hanged). In 1714 the Negroes were accused, very likely falsely, of attempting to burn the town. To make sure that it would not happen, fourteen Negroes were burned at the stake, eighteen were hanged, and seventy-one were transported.

More than a century had passed since Henry Hudson, in the employ of the burghers of Amsterdam, Holland, had been despondent over the fact that he had merely discovered a great river and not merchants in gems and silks. Much water—and much blood—had flowed to the ocean. There were wars and revolutions, and kings lost thrones and heads. The land changed masters and names, changed languages and contours. But a greater change still was gestating in the minds and hearts of men, not only in the New World but in the Old as well.

Indeed, it was the mother countries which were to feed ideas through the umbilical cord binding their peoples, and the daughter country was to put them into practice, give them the flesh and blood of reality.

Language is the translation of man's original weapons— fist, rock, club—and is still his most formidable arsenal. The tyrant first assaults man's language. Muzzle his mouth; destroy his tablets, his parchment, his books; break his stiles, his pens, his printing-presses. Silence! And with what pride the tyrant points to the hushed tranquility of his realm in contrast to the turbulence of a free democracy. As well might the monarch of a dead sea point disdainfully to the roaring waves of living waters.

Governor Fletcher brought William Bradford from Pennsylvania in 1693 to open the first printing establishment in New York. Bradford started the first newspaper, the weekly *New-York Gazette,* on November 8, 1725. Strange how many papers and magazines bear the name of "gazette"! Do their publishers know that the word is of Italian origin and means "little magpie" chatterer, babbler? Or, is it instinct which prompts them?

The *New-York Gazette* was not, however, the mouth which spoke the thoughts of man, but a hollowed space through which the words of the masters echoed and re-echoed. The people could no longer endure the stifling, and John Peter Zenger, a Palatine immigrant and former apprentice to Bradford, began issuing *The New York Weekly Journal*. The young German was a writer of ability and courage, and what he had to say did not please the Governor and his cohorts, who finally ordered that four numbers of the *Journal* be burned at the pillory by the common hangman, in the presence of mayor and aldermen; Zenger was arrested on charges of libel.

It looked pretty bad for the editor and the free press. A *deus ex machina*, in the shape of Andrew Hamilton of Philadelphia, octogenarian, and America's greatest lawyer, appeared in the courtroom where Zenger's fate was being decided and offered his services. "It is not the cause of a poor printer, nor of New York alone which you are trying," he said. "No! It is the best cause; it is the cause of liberty, both of exposing and opposing arbitrary power by speaking and writing truth!"

So overwhelming were his oratory and his arguments that the jury after only a few minutes of deliberation, brought out the verdict—"Not Guilty!" And the right of free press was established for all time. Again and again there were assaults upon it, to be sure, but the roots were solidly planted and the trunk grew tall and mighty. The axe of the muzzlers in every generation might scar it, but the scars healed and the tree stood.

There were a few other papers before the Revolution, but their editors were annoyed by the British, and only as the Republic was established do we begin to see the burgeoning of the press destined to blossom into the magnificent (despite all shortcomings and all evils) institution of today. In 1805 the State legislature enacted a law for the right to publish "truth with good motives and for justifiable ends, even though it reflects on the government."

But for a half-century after the Revolution, there were still crude, hand-driven presses and paper was difficult to procure, and the public was urged, as a patriotic duty, to save its scraps of paper and rags that papermaking might go on.

12 The War of Nerves

ZENGER'S victory was not definitive. The landlords in this State as well as the absentee lords in England might lose a battle but they were not ready to lose the war, and everywhere people began to grasp—vaguely at first—that this war was not merely against a certain man, a certain legislation, a local grievance, but the war for a new world—not only in the new world, but in the old, as well.

It was to be a longer and fiercer war than anyone living—however wise and clairvoyant—could foresee. And it is well they did not, for they might have lost heart or become disoriented. Battle by battle, skirmish by skirmish, a victory for hope, a defeat to gather anger—and when the day of decision came they were ready.

It was a weary and circuitous journey. They had to travel through dark tunnels of depression, climb steep hills of sacrifice clinging to creaking branches, and often it must have seemed like a foolish dream. And many must have remembered the Exodus, for they were mighty readers of the Bible. "And when Pharaoh drew nigh, the children of Israel lifted up their eyes, and, behold, the Egyptians marched after them; and they were sore afraid and . . . cried out. . . . For it had been better for us to serve the Egyptians, than that we should die in the wilderness."

To many it must have seemed that the leaders and their followers were but an army of Don Quixotes riding on famished nags, and there were many fat Sancho Panzas who ridiculed them, for Sancho Panzas love solid saddles underneath their fat buttocks. Yet there must also have been a scholar here and there who had read the works of that philosopher of Holland, Baruch de Spinoza, who warned that "all things excellent are as difficult as they are rare."

And some there were who had discovered the word "Liberty." A word is a banner. With it aloft man goes forth to martyrdom and to victory. A word is a challenge to evil, a torch in the night of slavery, a vision amid the squalor of quotidian reality, the essence of a thousand dreams.

Fifty years had to pass after Zenger for the great news to arrive, on April 23, 1775, that . . .

> . . . the embattled farmers stood
> And fired the shot heard round the world.

Not round the world as yet, but in due time.

Meanwhile, during the half-century, the population grew, the means of communication were extended and ramified, there were more riches and more poverty, and a constantly growing resentment at the evident fact that the colonies existed for the glory and the advancement of the mother country and in particular the Crown. It was not a mother but a stepmother.

Medievalism compounded with mercantilism, medievalism in the social structure and mercantilism in the economic. The rich landowners, who received their grants from the Crown, naturally tried their utmost to perpetuate the two. The leaseholder paid his rent in kind and labor was hired by contract for a term of years, while the evils of apprenticeship were unrelieved. Moreover, only freemen could practice trade or own shops, and 10 per cent of the population was Negro and slaves.

The English were ardent followers of the economic theory of mercantilism which, whatever merits it may have had for England, was ruinous to colonies. They were to provide raw materials not available at home and be a market for the finished goods of the home country. Whenever it suited her purposes, England raised high tariffs to exclude certain colonial products, or nip in the bud the development of colonial manufactures. She even forbade the exportation of particular goods from one colony to the other. Besides, all trading must be done in English boats or in foreign ships belonging to the nations involved, but never in colonial boats.

"Act" after "act" irritated the colonists and hardened the oppressors, who even resorted to the modern technique of dictators of corrupting the halls of learning, for in 1754 the Parliament chartered the first college in New York, King's College (now Columbia University), raised by public lotteries, "to prevent the growth of republican principles which already too much prevail in the colonies."

People suffer the yoke of tyrants for long periods and only move it a little higher or lower on their necks. Belts can be tightened notch after notch. Misery becomes almost a welcomed guest. Man does not rebel until his mind is fevered with the fire of freedom. Mind is man's great weapon. Thought is war. And there were many sparks in the wind now to enflame the mind.

There were the "Encyclopaedists," for example, rebel spirits of France, who set themselves, under the leadership of Diderot, to scheme out a new world. Their glory lay "in their hatred for all things unjust, in their denunciation of the trade in slaves, of the inequalities of taxation, of the corruption of justice, of the wastefulness of wars, in their dreams of social progress, in their sympathy with the rising empire of industry which was beginning to transform the world."

And there was James Otis who in 1762, already had these things to say:

God made all men naturally equal. Ideas of earthly superiority are educational, not innate. Kings were made for the good of the people, and not the people for them. No government has a right to make slaves of its subjects. Though most governments are *de facto* arbitrary, and consequently the curse and scandal of human nature, yet none are *de jure* arbitrary.

And there were other men—Thomas Paine, Benjamin Franklin, Patrick Henry, Thomas Jefferson, The Adamses, James Madison, Alexander Hamilton, George Washington. Their thoughts and their words fired the minds. The people became restive under the yoke, and the day was nearing when they would cast it to the ground, and stamp upon it.

The Revolution, of course, would not eliminate all the evils; nor, indeed, have they been entirely eliminated generations later, although names and masks conceal facts and faces. There is no cemetery where mankind may bury its forms of society as they outlive their usefulness, and the tombstones raised by historians are but fictitious ornaments to perpetuate man's illusion of constant progress. One society merges into another and what was discarded as débris may reappear as foundation. The dead are always with us and often bury the living.

The treaty of Paris in 1763 freed the colonies from dependence on the British for protection against the French and the Indians. The French no longer had any claims on that part of the Continent which eventually became the United States, and the Indians were placated, not to say liquidated. Now the colonies were ready to unite, but the British, goaded by greed and led by an incredibly stupid government and king, piled blunder upon blunder and inso-

lence upon insolence on a proud people whose ancestors had
been dissenters in religion and politics.

There was no question at first of complete rupture with
England. There was a demand to be treated as equals—perhaps not quite as equals. After all, this was a callow province
—how could it claim equality with that ancient, great nation?
This feeling of inferiority was to persist for at least a century beyond the Revolution certainly, in the arts, in manners, in speech, in culture. It was something to be praised by
an English critic; what lady would not have sacrificed her
virtue to be presented at the Court of St. James; what did it
mean to "put on the Ritz," if not to speak with a British
accent?

What the colonists wished was to be treated decently,
with a modicum of justice and consideration. It was a new
country but the people were grown up. They could not forever accept the mentorship of a parent whose claim to obedience was ancestral memories and pretension to affection
by blood. The blood had already begun to mix and the ancestral memories were growing dim and varied.

Already, in 1755, John Adams, then a school teacher in
Connecticut, wrote in his diary: "In another century all
Europe will not subdue us. The only way to keep us from
setting up for ourselves is to disunite us." That technique the
English employed and nearly won. However, remarks such
as Adams' were at first whispered, then hinted in newspapers
and pamphlets, and only as the war finally broke out, accepted as a fact.

In 1733, on top of all the other "acts," was passed the Im-
portation Act. New and exorbitant duties were laid on sugar,
molasses, and rum. In 1750 it was further enacted that iron-
works should not be erected in the colonies, and the manu-

facture of steel was specifically prohibited, as well as the felling of pines.

The colonists generally managed to circumvent these monstrosities, but the advent of George III, as king of England, meant a more strenuous effort to enforce these laws, and consequently further resistance. The colonial courts issued a search-warrant, the Writ of Assistance, which gave the authority to petty constables to enter any place and seize goods he suspected of having been smuggled without duty. And what is so irritating as a little man with a big stick?

Great Britain, though victorious in the long drawn-out French and Indian War, was deeply in debt. Why should not the colonies bear the brunt of the expenses, the ministers in the House of Commons demanded. Because, the colonies replied, England ought to defend her possessions; as a matter of fact, the colonies had aided England quite as much as England had aided the colonies; and the cession of Canada had amply rewarded England. And anyway, henceforth the American States would prefer to fight her own wars unaided.

As long as England believed the colonies too weak to retaliate, she would listen neither to the eloquence of William Pitt nor to the remonstrances of the colonists, and by a majority of five to one the House of Commons voted the infamous "Stamp Act."

Henceforth every note, bond, deed, mortgage, lease, license, legal document in the colonies had to be executed on paper bearing an English stamp, which was to be furnished by the British government. For each sheet the colonists were to pay from three pence to six pounds sterling. Every pamphlet, almanac, newspaper required the same sort of paper, while every advertisement was taxed two shillings.

"The sun of American liberty has set," Benjamin Franklin wrote to a friend. "Now we must light the lamps of industry

The Manhattan skyline, viewed from beneath the Brooklyn Bridge.

Visitors walk across a restored French drawbridge over a moat to enter Old Fort Niagara at Youngstown. The entrance gate, originally built in 1756, was named *Porte des Cinq Nations* in honor of the five Iroquois Indian nations.

The inner courtyard of Fort Ste. Marie de Gannentaha, near Syracuse. The reproduction of the fort, originally built in 1656, followed Jesuit plans still in existence in France.

View from Rondaxe Mountain in the Central Adirondack section.

Watkins Glen, a picturesque rock ravine with thirty-nine waterfalls.

Noon hour at the Sub-Treasury Building in Wall Street. The statue of George Washington commemorates the first President's inauguration on this site.

Boldt Castle, a tour boat stop in the Thousand Islands region.

Sunnyside, a restoration of Washington Irving's home between Irvington and Tarrytown in the lower Hudson River Valley.

Hasbrouck House in Newburgh served as George Washington's headquarters in 1782 and 1783.

An ornamental cannon on Mount Defiance marks the position where British troops placed guns to shell Fort Ticonderoga.

Built in 1772 as a church by the settlers of the Schoharie Valley, this building, now a museum, was converted into a fort for protection against British raiding parties during the Revolution. The tall stone monument near the flagpole identifies the grave of David Williams, one of the captors of Major André, the British agent who plotted with Benedict Arnold.

Philipse Castle, restoration of a building originally erected in 1683 in the Sleepy Hollow section of the Hudson River Valley.

Perrine's Bridge, near Rosendale in the Catskill Mountains, is the oldest covered bridge in New York State.

The State Capitol at Albany.

The Church of the Holy Trinity Monastery, near Jordanville, which has nine "golden domes."

A corner of the study at Quarry Farm, near Elmira, where Mark Twain did much of his writing.

A quaint hook windmill at East Hampton, Long Island.

Route 86A in the Keene Valley at the foot of the Adirondack Mountains.

The Ausable River, with Whiteface Mountain in the background.

A scene near Palatine Bridge in the Mohawk Valley region. The tug in the background is one of many in service on the Erie Canal, a branch of New York's Barge Canal system.

From Route 9 the motorist gets a glimpse of island-studded Lake George at the entrance to the Adirondack Mountains.

and economy." At this date he was still Poor Richard. His friend, whose vision was sharper, replied: "Be assured, that we shall light torches of another sort."

America was indignant and wrathful. In Philadelphia muffled bells tolled. In New York the Sons of Liberty, a group of young patriots carried placards with various legends: "The Folly of England and the Ruin of America," "The first Man that either distributes or makes use of Stampt Paper let him take care of His House, person and Effects."

On All Saints' Day the Sons of Liberty, followed by some hundreds of citizens, assembled on the Common, or Fields, now City Hall Park, where they improvised a gallows and hanged in effigy Cadwallader Colden, lieutenant-governor and chief representative of royal authority in New York. The mob then formed a torch-light procession and, gibbet and all, marched down Broadway to the fort, placed the gibbet against the door, and hammered the door with clubs. General Thomas Gage, commander-in-chief, had strengthened the garrison, but as yet he was not ready to order the soldiers to shoot upon the citizens.

Fired with confidence, they broke open the governor's coachhouse, dragged out his chariot, put the effigy within it, tore the wooden fence which enclosed the Bowling Green, and made a bonfire of all and sundry. Colden watched and the garrison waited, but no orders were given. Cowardice saveth the skin of the mighty.

A part of the crowd continued its itinerary by going to pay a visit to Major Thomas James, commandant at Fort George, who had boasted that he would "cram the stamps down the rebel throats." His residence was on the corner of the present Warren and Greenwich Streets, and filled with rich furniture. They looted it and made another bonfire.

Meanwhile, legal business was almost entirely suspended.

The courthouses were closed. Even marriage licenses could not be issued. The importers of New York, Boston, and Philadelphia entered into a solemn pact to boycott all British goods until the Stamp Act was repealed.

Across the ocean, the wealthy citizens of the Tight Little Island were highly indignant. What, those barbarians dared thwart their plans! Why did not the army fire upon the rebels? Treason, that's what it was, treason, treason! But there were tradesmen and manufacturers who knew their interests and sided with the Americans, and there was still Mr. Pitt who, though ill, made a powerful address. "You have no right to tax America. I rejoice that America has resisted. Three millions of our fellow-subjects so lost to every sense of virtue as tamely to give up their liberties would be fit instruments to make slaves of the rest."

On the 18th of March, 1766, the Stamp Act was formally repealed. What jubilation! The vessels on the Thames were decked with flags and the colonial orators, prototypes of the later political campaigners, orated on the majesty of His Majesty.

In New York bells rang, cannons boomed, bonfires blazed, and on the birthday of the king, the 4th of June, the people celebrated by roasting an ox whole and erecting a pole with the inscription: "The King, Pitt, and Liberty." They petitioned the assembly to erect a statue to Pitt. The assembly went one further, and voted also an equestrian statue to the king to be set in the Bowling Green. Pitt in a Roman toga had his head knocked off and his arms amputated by the British soldiers during the Revolution. It now lies in peace in the halls of the New York Historical Society.

The joy was of short duration, for His Majesty and the officeholders and the landlords on both sides of the ocean had by no means given up the idea of squeezing the juicy fruit which was the New World. On the 29th of June, 1767, an act was passed, therefore, imposing a duty on all the glass, paper, papers' colors, and tea imported into the colonies. As if this were not enough, Parliament adopted a resolution suspending the general assembly of New York until it should vote the full cost of the soldiers' upkeep in the State.

Now the statue of the king became the symbol of tyranny and the Sons of Liberty, once more active, raised the "liberty pole" on the Common. And the war of nerves went on.

13 *Interlude*

MEANWHILE the people, by a very ancient habit, continued to live and multiply. By the time of the Revolution New York had a population of twenty thousand, not a mean number in those days of epidemics which decimated nations. Building went on apace. There was a continuous line of wharves and docks and shipyards all along the river front. Broadway beyond the Common continued to be a grassy lane for a while yet, but above the Collect and along the Bowery Lane, there were the country seats, and Greenwich was becoming a village of importance. The most imposing structure was the City Hall, which had replaced the Stadt Huys in 1700. The mayor had his office here and here were held the meetings of the common council and the provincial assembly, and the courts dispensed justice.

Then there was the Merchants' Exchange, a brick structure on arches, between Water and Front Streets, and associated with it there were markets. One was on Liberty Street, another on Fulton Street, and lesser ones at the foot of every thoroughfare. But to what use closing a deal if one cannot have a drink or a bite to celebrate the occasion, and so taverns and coffee-houses opened doors and arms. There was King's Arms and Black Horse and Queen's Head, and, at the present 181st Street and Broadway, the Blue Bell Tavern for weary travelers. The Province Arms had "stables and all things necessary for the entertainment of travelers."

Among entertainments the theater was an established feature. The beginning of the eighteenth century already witnessed professional actors doing their stunts in New York. Alas, their names are recorded on no scroll of honor! Shakespeare would have been even more accurate had he said instead of "Frailty—thy name's woman," "Frailty—thy name's the actor's glory." A painter may have his work exhibited hundreds of years after his demise; a composer may have his piece played centuries after his poor bones have rotted in Potter's field; an author may be read even after the language he wrote in is understood by university bookworms only, but an actor is forever dead the minute the applause ceases, and must be resurrected with every performance. There is no attic for discarded mummers.

Around the middle of the century, however, one begins to read in the newspapers news of the stage. "Last week," the *Weekly Post Boy* of February 26, 1750 reports, "arrived here a company of comedians from Philadelphia, who we hear have taken a convenient room for the purpose in one of the buildings lately belonging to the Hon. Rip Van Dam, Esq., deceased, where they intend to perform as long as the season lasts, provided they meet with suitable encouragement." Admission to the gallery was three shillings and to the pit five, the performance starting "at precisely half an hour after six o'clock, and no person being admitted behind the scenes."

Thereafter New York was never without its company or companies, both American and English, and several theaters were built, the most popular being the one which housed the Hallam Company on the north side of John Street between Broadway and Nassau Street—a wooden structure, painted red, with a pit, two rows of boxes and a gallery. The company was conducted cooperatively: eighteen shares—four for the plant, three for the manager, and one for each actor. The venture was successful and Hallam retired rich.

The plays offered were generally the tragedies of Shakespeare, the comedies of Congreve, Goldsmith, and Farquhar. The audience was critical and, despite the shabbiness of costumes and scenery, the performances were adequate. Negro slaves in livery were sent to procure seats in advance, and ladies came to the theater in chariots or sedan chairs.

The eighteenth century was the "age of reason," and Deism and atheism were in the air, but New York was essentially a church-going community, with the Reformed Dutch the most numerous sect even in the second half of the century. There were several structures built between 1693 when the church was within the fort and the new century—one on Garden Street, one on Nassau, one on the west side of William. The Huguenot church, a low stone building, erected in 1704, stood on the north side of Pine Street. The Friends' Meeting House, a small wooden building, was situated midway between Broadway and Liberty Place. The Lutherans had a steepleless church on the corner of William and Frankfort Streets. The Presbyterians had their place of worship between Broadway and Nassau Streets. The Moravian church was built on the south side of Fulton. The Baptist church stood on the west side of Gold. German Calvinists held services in a former theater on Nassau Street. The Methodists built their first chapel in 1768 between Nassau and William Streets. The Jews built their first synagogue in 1730 on the north side of Mill Street, now vanished. The Catholics had no church as yet.

Most of the churches were flanked by burying-grounds, while the cemetery of the Jews occupied a plot bounded by Chatham, Catherine, and Olive Streets.

Illiteracy was rampant. There was a charity school under

the care of Trinity Church, and another connected with the Dutch, but like all charitable institutions, much more apt to stultify the mind than uplift it. The rich had their private tutors or went abroad to gather a little knowledge and much vanity.

King's College, a three-story building bounded by Church, Murray, and Barclay Streets, put on a good fight in the name of education. The first graduating class, 1758, consisted of eight students, but next year only one student received his degree of Bachelor of Arts.

Another laudable institution was the fire department. There were two fire engines; each one "required twelve men to work it, took water from a cistern, or, failing that, from a wooden trough, into which water was poured, and could throw a continuous jet seventy feet high, and with such a velocity as to break windows." There were, therefore, twenty-four firemen, who received no money but were exempt from other public duties. When an alarm was sounded they dragged the engine to the fire and there, under the direction of the magistrates, "with the utmost diligence, manage, work and play the said fire-engines and all other tools and instruments, at such fire with all their power, skill, strength and understanding; and when the fire was out shall draw the engine back."

The streets of the City were generally unpaved, narrow, and filled with litter, as were also the great capitals of Europe, Paris, London, Vienna. Cleanliness was still after godliness, and godliness limped behind Mammon.

"And God made two great lights; the greater light to rule the day, and the lesser light to rule the night: he made the stars also." And the citizens of New York depended upon the "lesser light" to brighten their paths, but when the "lesser light" absented itself or was blanketed by clouds,

they were required to hang out a lantern on the end of a
pole from the window of every seventh house—the mystical
number of Genesis and dice.

There was also a night watch of a score of men, whose
habitat was the basement of the City Hall, doubtless convinced that evil unseen is evil nonexistent.

The Dutch had left their solid imprint upon the architecture of the City.

Most of the houses are of brick and several stories high. Some
have the gable and towards the street, but the new are altered in
this respect. Many of the houses have a balcony on the roof, in
which the people sit in the summer evenings. These roofs are
covered with tiles or shingles of wood. The walls are covered
with all sorts of drawings and pictures in small frames. On each
side of the chimney they usually have an alcove, and the wall
under the windows wainscoted, and have benches placed under it.

The rich had great gardens around their homes, which
were built for comfort and posterity and filled with imported
furniture. Togged in silks and satins and sporting swords,
they traveled in huge coaches attended by liveried postillions
and outriders, while their wives and mistresses, blazing with
jewels, engaged in the ancient game of gossip and scandal.

The future Empire State was, for the time being, centered
in the future Metropolis, but there were other towns which
were destined to become populous and wealthy and famed
for culture, science, industry, politics.

There was Albany—oldest of the permanent European
settlements in the United States. As early as 1610, trading
houses were built on the site to traffic with the Indians. It
continued as a focal point on the River and in 1754 was
sufficiently important throughout the colonies to be chosen
as the meeting place for the representatives to arrange for

a permanent union. Less than a half-century later it became the capital of the State.

There was Schenectady, seventeen miles northwest of Albany, originally the chief village of the Mohawk Indians and settled in 1662 by Arendt Van Corlear.

There was Buffalo, visited in 1679 by La Salle, at one time named New Amsterdam but changed to the present name because of the herds of bison frequenting the salt licks near by.

There was germination in all the land through which the Great River flowed, from where it is "a minute, unpretending tear of the clouds" to where it merges with the ocean.

14 Divorce

THERE were those who buried their heads in the sands of wishful thinking, forgetting that their rears were exposed and vulnerable. There were those who talked about the marriage between lions and lambs; but only lions dream of possessing lambs, lambs much preferring their permanent state of celibacy. There were those who, jaundiced with inertia, wrapped themselves with sanctimonious shawl of patience and "God knows best." There were those who with "philosophic" disdain spoke of enjoying one's self today, for tomorrow one may be dead. And there were those, who had vision and guts and who said openly, "you can't do business with England."

And soon they were proved right, for England once again came to the assault. This time the packets from London brought the news that she would force her colonies to pay the tea tax. More than tea was involved, for if the colonists were coerced and fooled into paying the tax on tea, sooner or later other articles would be placed on the list. The question was "taxation without representation," or a people's right to self-government, for they who pull the purse-strings pull the strings which make the people dance to their tunes.

The English employed tricks and ruses and threats, their usual arsenal of weapons, but the colonists had reached a saturation point. The first evidence of this took place in a skirmish between the citizens of Boston and soldiers. The soldiers, exasperated by the hooting and the taunts of the civilians, discharged a volley, killing three and wounding several more. This "Boston Massacre" convinced many who still believed in compromise and appeasement that the English were ready, if necessary, to go the limit to remain the masters of the colonies.

Lord North proclaimed, "To repeal the tea duty would stamp us with timidity," and to prove that he meant what he said he framed a number of acts which would make of rebellious Massachusetts an example to all the others. One act closed the port of Boston. A second suspended the charter of the colony. A third provided for the quartering of troops within the province. A fourth legalized the transfer to England of trials due to riots.

George III signed the acts "with supreme satisfaction," despite the warnings of Burke, Barré and Fox, men who saw farther than their noses.

If the English considered this an entering wedge between the colonies, a clever piece of "divide and rule," they were much mistaken. Rather it proved to be cement. People are not united by love but by a common hate against a common enemy. Christopher Gadsden of South Carolina sent his message to the Bostonians, "Don't pay for an ounce of their damned tea." Colonel George Washington, of Virginia, was ready to raise and head an army of a thousand men at his own expense to march to the relief of the town. The Sons of Liberty of New York proposed a Continental Congress. Instantly the proposal was accepted by all the colonies, with the exception of Georgia.

John Jay, a young lawyer of Huguenot descent, headed the New York delegation which assembled in Philadelphia and was one of the framers of a declaration of colonial rights, claiming for the people of America, "a free and exclusive power of legislation in their provincial legislatures, where their rights of legislation could alone be preserved in all cases of taxation and internal polity." Ah, if tyrants were wise or wise men were rulers! But George III and his flatterers were not wise, and the wise men of England did not have the power, and the conclusion was inevitable.

The First Congress, besides adopting the resolution, pledged to import no goods from England and the West Indies and set a date for the second meeting.

England, with bulldog obstinacy, continued to send ships loaded with tea for the American market. Some vessels reached Charleston and managed to land the tea, but the people forbade its sale. New York and Philadelphia were closed ports. At Boston the vessels entered the harbor, but the authorities would not allow the tea to be landed.

Seven thousand people gathered in a town-meeting and listened to fiery speakers, including Adams and Quincy. As the meeting was about to adjourn, a war-whoop was heard, and fifty "Indians" were wending their way to Griffin's wharf where the boats lay at anchor. The meeting broke and a crowd followed the embattled ones, who boarded the vessels, broke open the chests of tea and poured the contents into the sea. And this gesture of defiance was the gauntlet thrown in the face of tyranny.

In September 1774, the Second Colonial Congress, also known as the First Continental Congress, assembled at Philadelphia. Eleven of the colonies were represented. It was unanimously agreed that Massachusetts should be sustained in her struggle against the cruel oppressors. A copy of the resolution was sent to the king, another directly to the English nation and a third to the people of Canada. These were the days when the people, as distinct from their governments, began to have significance. The divine right of kings was soon to be considered neither divine nor right. The Bill of Rights and the Declaration of the Rights of Man were to be promulgated before the end of the century.

Furthermore, the First Colonial Congress adopted the recommendation to suspend all trading with Great Britain until she redressed the wrongs she had perpetrated upon the colonies. And Parliament answered in its usual blind and arrogant manner. It ordered General Gage, recently appointed governor of Massachusetts, to force a showdown. To aid him in this, they despatched a fleet and ten thousand soldiers. The governor ordered the assembly to disband. The members countered by forming themselves into a provincial congress and voted to equip an army of twelve thousand men.

In New York, meanwhile, the half-Royalist assembly adjourned, never to meet again, and a provincial congress was established. Events were galloping and the tempo was martial. Names appeared now which were destined to become immortal. There was the seventeen-year-old King's College student, Alexander Hamilton, who was making stirring speeches on the Common. In another twelvemonth, Thomas Paine would publish his *Common Sense,* a non-fiction bestseller. Nathan Hale would hang for his devotion to his country. And there were Thomas Jefferson and George Washington.

General Gage ordered Boston Neck seized and fortified and the military arsenals in Cambridge and Charleston taken to Boston. His mask dropped; the people saw the hideous face of the conqueror and the tyrant's tool. Immediately they concealed their ammunition in rubbish wagons and removed them to Concord.

Gage despatched a regiment of soldiers to destroy the stores. But while the soldiers were on the march, Paul Revere

on his faithful mare (if mare it was), galloped to immortal
legend. Bells rang, cannons fired. The people of America
awakened to battle and to freedom.

Events were galloping in New York as well. On March
5, 1775, a pitched battle "took place between the Whigs
and the Tories; the latter defeated," and on April 3, the
Assembly adjourned, never to meet again. By order of the
Committee of Safety, the militia recently formed under the
name of "Hearts of Oak," went to remove the cannons from
the Battery. The seventy-four gun ship, *Asia*, anchored off
the fort, sent a broadside into them, killing one.

On April 24 a horseman dashed furiously into the city and
relayed the news of the battle of Lexington. The Sons of
Liberty, under the command of Samuel Broome, at last re-
lieved of the tension induced by the moderates who still
preached caution, dashed to City Hall, took possession of
it, as well as of the war matériel stored there. "They demanded and obtained the key to the Custom House; closed
the building and laid an embargo upon the vessels in port
destined for the eastern colonies."

On May 5, at a meeting held in the Coffee House, a pro-
visional government for the City was formed, "and the people pledged themselves to obey its orders until different
arrangements should be made by the Continental Congress."

The Committee, however, was not of one mind, and there
were still among them those who would traffic with the
enemy. Not only carriers of umbrellas, but danglers of
swords have been appeasers since time immemorial.

There was also the question of the press. John Holt, editor
of the *New York Journal* and city postmaster, was the sturdy
spokesman of the Sons of Liberty. The heading of his paper
had once been the arms of the king, but these he discarded,
and used instead a snake cut into parts, with the legend:

"Unite or Die." The next year the snake was joined and coiled, with tail in mouth, forming a double ring, enclosing a pillar standing on Magna Carta, surmounted with the cap of liberty.

Holt was compelled to flee the city when the English entered. However, he took the press with him, and continued to publish under very hazardous conditions. He died soon after the conclusion of peace. In St. Paul's churchyard one may still see his tomb with epitaph:

A due tribute to the memory of John Holt, printer to this State, a native of Virginia, who patiently obeyed death's awful summons on the 13th of January, 1784, in the sixty-fourth year of his age. To say that his family lament him is needless; that his friends bewail him, is useless; that all regret him, unnecessary; for that he merited every esteem is certain. The tongue of slander cannot say less, though justice might say more.

But different, indeed, is the story of James Rivington, editor of the *Gazetteer and Weekly Advertiser,* the organ of the Royalists. His attacks upon the patriots became so vicious, that the Sons of Liberty broke open the door of his office, in Wall Street, destroyed his press, and carried off his type.

Rivington went to England and returned in 1777 with a new press and new type and published the *Royal Gazette* until the close of the war. When it became evident that the English would be defeated, he quietly turned spy for Washington, for which reason he was allowed to live unmolested after the colonists gained their independence. He died in penury and oblivion, which is not always the "happy ending" of scoundrels and traitors.

And there was also the little matter of education and educators. King's College chartered "to prevent the growth of republican principles," was in proper hands. Myles Cooper, the president, was a Royalist with a big mouth. His opinions had finally so enraged the Sons of Liberty that, on the night of August 23, a crowd set out for the hall of learning to prove to the false scholar that the tongue is the rope wherewith many hang themselves.

Alexander Hamilton, however, faithful to his Alma Mater, mounted the stoop and upbraided them, "on the excessive impropriety of their conduct and the disgrace they were bringing to the cause of liberty, of which they professed to be the champions." Another student, equally faithful, had meanwhile warned the prexy, who escaped over the college fence and the next day boarded the *Asia* and returned to England. The college, some months later, serving no purpose closed its doors until the end of hostilities.

And so came the Revolution. Once the Dutch, fat-bottomed, had no heart for fight and lost one colony. More than a century later the English, fat-headed, had no heart for those oppressed and lost thirteen colonies which, freed, developed into the mightiest of nations.

On April 14, 1776, Washington arrived from Boston to make New York his headquarters. He took up residence on Richmond Hill, on the corner of Varick and Charlton Streets until he retreated from the city and fixed his headquarters at Robert Murray's house on Murray Hill.

At the time of Washington's residence, Richmond Hill fronted the Hudson with nothing to obstruct the view.

Meadows stretched up toward the little hamlet of Greenwich Village, and on the left the view of the little city in the distance was half hidden by clumps of trees and rising hills. There was a broad entrance to the house, under a porch of imposing height supported by high columns, with balconies fronting the rooms of the second story. The premises were entered by a spacious gate-

way, flanked by ornamental columns, at what is now the termi-
nation of Macdougal Street. Within the gate and to the north was
a beautiful sheet of water known as Burr's pond.

Richmond Hill remained a spot of glory for a long time
after Washington's residence, being also Vice President
Adams' home for one year and thereafter Aaron Burr's. The
evil which later befell Burr was reflected in the house as
well, and it gradually lost its glamour, became a theater, a
circus, a menagerie, and was abandoned.

There were great many more patriots than people who
thoroughly grasped the meaning of the struggle between
Gage's men and the colonists. It was still a family squabble,
and disobedience to the Big Father in London was still felt
as treason. There was talk of divorce but hope of reconcili-
ation. No umbilical cord is severed with such reluctance as
apron strings. The man whose words were the sharp shears
had only been in this country three years, but he saw more
clearly and farther than any of his contemporaries, and his
book, *Common Sense,* galvanized the nation. There was
luminous intelligence, logic unanswerable, pride of spirit,
courage, and the urgency of liberty that had gripped the
whole western world.

Meanwhile, the First Congress had awaited for a half-year
His Majesty's reply to the American grievances, and when it
came it was typical—the reply tyrants always make to those
who use words instead of bullets. Contemptuously, the king
denied the existence of a Continental Congress and ordered
it as well as the army disbanded. Unconditional surrender.
Then, in his magnanimity, the king would settle all questions
with each colony separately.

Came the Divorce. On the Fourth of July, 1776, at two
o'clock in the afternoon, the Second Continental Congress of

America adopted the Declaration of American Independence by a unanimous vote. And the bell in the steeple of the State House in Philadelphia rang out, and the whole world was destined to hear it—some places sooner, some places later, but all would hear it.

15 *Travail*

THE Declaration of Independence was ratified unanimously by the Provincial Congress of New York on July 9th. That evening several brigades of the army reported to their parade grounds, and in the presence of George Washington an aide read the Declaration. The soldiers cheered, and to spread the joy all debtors were released from prison. Headed by Isaac Sears, the Sons of Liberty marched down Broadway and pulled down the leaden statue of George III on Bowling Green and chopped it. Why Washington should have been angry at this can only be explained by a remnant of unconscious reverence for the erstwhile Pater. It is difficult not to confound greatness with size, eminence with pedestal and sanctity with robe.

Forty-two thousand ball cartridges were manufactured from the carcass, and Washington registered no further objection.

On the 22nd of August Lord Howe landed his troops on Long Island, and New York found itself the center of operations. The Hudson River was the key of Britain's strategy. They used it as a wedge dividing our New England forces from those of the South. For this reason, Washington countered by trying at all costs to prevent the complete fulfillment of the foe's objective. Indeed, he kept as many troops as he could on the River in order to strike now east, now

south. No other area of the country saw as much of the con-
flict as New York and the valley of the River.

Howe tried conciliatory measures at first. They dealt
largely with amnesties and matters of small moment now to
the Americans who had already felt the baptism of blood
and fire. Washington replied that, the colonies being independent, they would defend themselves against all aggres-
sion.

Boat after boat belched the red-coats on the shores of
Gravesend; the battle of Long Island was a crushing defeat
for the colonial troops and Brooklyn was soon also lost. Two
thousand men were killed and three of the best officers made
prisoner. It seemed to Howe that he was within reach of victory, but a heavy fog came to the aid of the rebels, and when
it lifted Washington's entire force had disappeared from
Brooklyn Heights, had rowed across to Manhattan and
safety. Temporary safety only, for it was painfully evident
to Washington and Putnam that the British officer could in
one pincer movement both capture their armies and end the
war ingloriously. Had Howe, indeed, been more intent upon
his business than upon his luncheon at Mrs. Murray's, of
Murray Hill, he would have succeeded, but as it happened
the American armies escaped the trap, retaining the upper
end of the island. It was at this juncture, too, that the school
teacher swung to glory as he pronounced the essence of
patriotism: "I only regret that I have but one life to give for
my country!"

Synchronizing with the report of Nathan Hale's execution,
great fires began raging in various parts of captured New
York. It started in a small wooden house on the wharf near
the Whitehall Slip. "It was then occupied by a number of
men and women of a bad character." The two fire engines
evidently were out of order, or perhaps, the twenty-four men

who were to handle them were in uniform fighting the fire of tyranny.

The fire raged on, burning all the houses on the east side of Whitehall Slip and the west side of Broad Street to Beaver Street. Toward morning, the wind changing, the flames crossed Broadway to Beaver Lane, consuming all the houses on both sides of Broadway as well as some houses in New Street to Rector, and to John Harrison's three-story brick house, which stopped the fire on the east side of Broadway. It continued, however, burning all the houses in Lumber Street and all the houses on the west side of Broadway to St. Paul's Church. It reduced to ashes all the houses on both sides of Partition Street, and it did not stop until it reached Barclay Street. The college yard and the vacant ground finally put an end of it. Trinity Church was leveled, as well as the Lutheran Church, but St. Paul's Church escaped destruction. All in all 493 houses were destroyed, about one-tenth of the city's dwellings.

The Sons of Liberty were accused by Howe as incendiaries and a number of them thrown into the flames. Other citizens were thrown into prison but later released. "A Mr. White, a decent citizen and house carpenter, rather too violent a loyalist, and latterly had addicted himself to liquor, was on the night of the fire hanged on a tavern signpost, at the corner of Cherry and Roosevelt Streets."

The distress among the inhabitants was extreme. "They tacked sheets of canvas to the remnants of charred walls and standing chimneys, thus forming a city of tents, in which they bivouacked."

Two years later, another fire razed to the ground about three hundred buildings in the region south of Pearl Street, between Coenties and Old Slips. "Scarcely had the flames been quenched when a new calamity occurred"—the explosion of the powder ship Morning Star, which was anchored in the East River, during a violent thunderstorm.

But the worst calamity of all was the presence of the British troops. For several years it was under the heel of the cruel invader, lost more than half of its population and all of its commerce. Property belonging to the Royalists was marked and protected; all other confiscated by the Crown. The cost of living skyrocketed. Landlords constantly increased their rents, as houses became scarce both because of the fires and because no attempt was made to repair them or build new ones. Some of the necessities of life soared 800 per cent above normal prices. And the city became a city of prisons.

No sooner did the British capture the City than they converted every available building into a jail to house five thousand patriot soldiers, captured at Long Island and Fort Washington, whose ranks were steadily swelled by patriots not in uniform. The Middle Dutch Church furnished room for three thousand prisoners; the North Dutch Church another thousand; The Brick Huguenot, and Lutheran churches were used for a similar purpose, as well as Van Cortlandt's and Rhinelander's sugar-houses.

Adolph Meyer, of Lasher's battalion, one of the prisoners, writes about the brutal treatment accorded them.

Many prisoners died of want. No care was taken of the sick; and if any died, and they were thrown at the door of the prison, and lay there till the next day, when they were put on a cart and drawn out to the intrenchments, where they were buried by their fellow-prisoners, conducted thither for the purpose.

I have had men die by the side of me in the night [another captive writes], and I have seen fifteen dead bodies sewn up in their blankets and laid in the corner of the yard at one time. Once I was permitted to go with the guard to the place of internment, and never shall I forget the scene that I there beheld. They tum-

bled them into the ditch, threw on a little dirt, and then away.
I could see a hand, a foot, or part of a head, swollen and falling
into decay.

[Colonel Ethan Allen, also a prisoner, wrote] I have gone into
a church, and seen sundry of the prisoners in the agonies of death
in the consequence of very hunger, and others speechless and
near death, biting pieces of chip; others pleading for God's sake
for something to eat, and at the same time shivering with cold.
Hollow groans saluted my ears, and despair seemed imprinted on
every countenance. I have seen in these churches seven dead at
the same time.

Similar atrocities were perpetrated by the invaders on the
inmates jammed into the Old Provost Prison, whose keeper,
William Cunningham, was a renegade Son of Liberty. Starvation, disease, death, gradually cleared the churches, but
Old Provost Prison persisted in its horrible function until the
end of the war. Friends were denied admission, supplies were
stolen, doctors were driven away. But more disgraceful still
were the prison ships. A dozen hulks were moored and used
in succession as floating dungeons, the most notorious of
which, christened *Jersey*, was rechristened by the inmates
the hell afloat.

Often as many as a thousand prisoners were confined on
her, guarded by Hessians who laughed at their sufferings,
even as their fellow countrymen a century and three-quarters later laughed at the sufferings of the millions whom they
threw into concentration camps.

Thousands were buried from the prison ships in the shallow pits at the water's edge, where the tide uncovered their
graves. Later, their bones were recovered from the slime and
buried in cemeteries, many in Trinity churchyard.

New York became the headquarters of the British, and the
blood of the Americans being transmuted into gold rattling

in their purses, they sought and managed to squeeze some gaiety out of the butchery mess. Theaters and taverns were at their disposals, and there were tradesmen who trafficked with the foe, and also became rich. But the average inhabitant found life anything but gay. Washington fought no more engagements within the limits of New York, but there was still the fear that the Indians might swoop upon the city as in ancient days, and there were forays by our troops into Staten Island and skirmishes in the region of Kingsbridge, and who could tell when another fire, caused by reprisal or negligence, might devour the wooden buildings.

Meanwhile the patriot forces overran the countryside and cut off supplies to the city, and black markets flourished, but the poor had to resort to charity and lotteries to obtain food. On December 22, 1777, the *Weekly Mercury* writes:

On Wednesday next, being Christmas-eve, forty poor widows, housekeepers having families in this city, will receive forty pounds of fresh beef and half a peck loaf each, on a certificate of their necessity signed by two neighbors of repute, which is to be determined at the Rev. Dr. Inglis's house on Broadway, between ten and twelve o'clock that day, who will give a ticket for the above donation.

But the winter of 1779–1780 spared neither rich nor poor. "It exceeded in severity anything that had ever been dreamed of," says an old manuscript. "Wood was not to be had at any price, and many families would split up their chairs and tables to cook their breakfast, then go to bed for the rest of the day to keep warm. The rivers about the city were transformed into a solid of ice for forty days." And meanwhile, the battle against man was not forgotten, for the manuscript continues: "Eighty cannon were dragged across to Staten

Island from the foot of Rector Street to repel the expected attack of Lord Stirling."

The British commander sent his men to try to persuade the farmers to bring their products into town, but the farmers, fearful that they would be used to supply the enemy's forces, would hide their corn and oats beneath the snow and seek refuge with their cattle in the forests. Angered, the soldiers would set fire to homesteads and destroy entire districts. Still, the patriots, deeply immersed in the Bible, considering no Lord over them except God, proclaimed "that the land should be made a desert before it should be surrendered to a king."

The Grasshopper of a Tyrant continued to sing, unmindful of the evil day which would overcome him. Sir Henry Clinton who succeeded Howe as commander-in-chief, had his headquarters in the Kennedy house at the lower end of Broadway. There were balls and dinners, and the glittering uniform of the officers attracted the eyes of the wives and daughters of the loyalists—not loyal to their country, not loyal to the ideal of liberty which stirred the hearts of men, but loyal to a ruthless king, to a cruel aristocracy, to profit.

Meanwhile the patriots, under their great Chief, fought and bled and starved, and often their energies mutinied: "You have done enough! You cannot do any more! Go home! Call it quits! Make peace with the enemy! He cannot be worse than hunger and cold and open wounds!" But somehow they stuck. Somehow, despite all, they continued the struggle. Somehow, they had that last ounce of strength, of courage, of obstinacy, which in the end brings victory.

Meanwhile, too, we succeeded, thanks to the inimitable Benjamin Franklin, in negotiating a treaty of peace and commerce with the French king whose own days were numbered. He and his ministers were very wary of dealing openly with us, although they hated Britain and wished to see her defeat, for after all, who were we but the spiritual children of Voltaire and Rousseau and Diderot, and what was our ultimate aim if not to sweep off the face of the earth the ancient rot, including themselves? But the great charm, the sharp tongue, the wisdom, the gallantry of "Papa" Franklin, coupled with the news of Burgoyne's surrender, convinced Louis XVI, and on the 6th of February, 1778, he signed a treaty acknowledging the independence of the United States.

A half-year later there seemed a promise that the war would be over and New York escape her yoke, but it proved Fata Morgana's mirage. A powerful French fleet, commanded by Count d'Estaing, arrived at the Hook, while George Washington was once again encamped at White Plains. A joint attack was planned, and the defeat of the British army seemed certain, but the French admiral claimed that his flagship could not enter the harbor safely, commands were mixed, and the British remained for three more years.

In the autumn of 1781, Cornwallis surrendered his army at Yorktown, and in March 1782 Lord North and his associates resigned. His successor, Lord Rockingham, sent Sir Guy Carleton to New York to succeed Clinton and to negotiate for an early treaty of peace. On November 30, "after much correspondence and negotiation, preliminary articles of peace were signed at Paris, though intrigue was used by the British ambassadors to prevail on the American commissioners to accept a twenty years' truce, instead of an open acknowledgment of independence."

The British comprehended neither the temper of the people nor the temper of the times. How could they see, blinders of prejudice and greed obstructing their vision, that a half-dozen years later the French Revolution would, even more

than the American Revolution, proclaim the equality and
fraternity of all men—a revolution whose aims have not yet
been exhausted.

On September 3, 1783, a treaty definitive on the part of
Great Britain, recognizing the absolute independence of the
American States with all their material claims to rights and
territory, was signed.

On November 3, 1783, the Continental army was disbanded
by order of Congress, and on the 19th Washington arrived
at Day's Tavern, at the corner of One Hundred and Twenty-
fifth Street and Eighth Avenue. The enemy and their collaborators, however, lingered on until the 25th of the month
to take leave and left as sore-heads. They who always prate
about good sportsmanship were guilty of "many base and
unmanly outrages," among which, "unreeving the halyards
at Fort George, they knocked off the cleats and greased the
pole, to prevent the hoisting of the American colors; then
evacuated the fort, sure that the Stars and Stripes would not
be hoisted until they were far out of sight of their folds."
However, Goelet's hardware store in Hanover Square, supplied "the necessary tools to bore new cleats for the flagstaff,
and, with a sailor boy tying the halyards around his waist
and nailing the cleats above him to the right and left as he
ascended, the flag was hoisted to its place with a salute of
thirteen guns, heard by the British troops."

The collaborators, more fearful of their hides than con-
cerned about the welfare of their fellow citizens, were anxious to leave. Sir Guy Carleton offered them transportation
to Canada, where they were granted lands. Several thousand went to River St. John, other thousands to Port Rose-
way, Annapolis, and Halifax, and the remainder to Port
Moulton and Cumberland. But, like the British soldiers, they

belly-ached when they could no longer plunder or rejoice. William Bayard, one of the dignitaries of commerce, wrote to General Haldimand, commanding in Canada:

The shocking alteration in this once happy country and the good people of it since I had the honor of taking your excellency by the hand, owing to the wicked, infamous, and unprovoked rebellion, it is not possible to commit to paper nor tongue to express,— and the peace, as it is termed, worse than all both for poor old England and the king's truly loyal friends in this country. The rebels—for I shall never call them anything else—have confiscated every shilling of my valuable property in this country and passed an act of attainder against my person, so that I am now going off in a manner a beggar to my children and friends in old England, the reflection almost too shocking for human nature to bear; but such is mine and the hard fate of many others.

It was good riddance, for these people would have been a cancer in the frail new nation.

On November the 25th, at eight o'clock in the evening, General Knox commanding, the Continentals marched from McGowan's Pass down the old Post Road into the Bowery and halted; then into Chatham and into Queen Street, up Wall Street to Broadway and Rector Street.

The British and Hessians putting off to sea, an eyewitness wrote,

were as if equipped for show, and, with their scarlet uniforms and burnished arms, made a brilliant display; the troops that marched in, on the contrary, were ill-clad and weather-beaten, and made a forlorn appearance; but they were our troops; and as I looked at them and thought upon all they had done and suffered for us, my heart and my eyes were full, and I admired and gloried in them the more because they were weather-beaten and forlorn.

The incubus was lifted from the chest of the city. General Knox with a number of the prominent citizens on horseback repaired to the Bowery to receive His Excellency General Washington and the Governor of the State, George Clinton, who "with their respective suites, and followed by the Lieutenant Governor and Senators, the officers and citizens, on horseback, eight abreast, and citizens on foot, four abreast, entered the city through the Bowery, Chatham and Pearl Streets, to the Battery."

A few days of rest and celebration, and on December 4th, at Fraunces' Tavern, Washington took farewell of his officers. In his memoirs Colonel Benjamin Talmadge writes:

We had been assembled but a few moments when his excellency entered the room. His emotion, too strong to be concealed, seemed to be reciprocated by every officer present. After partaking of a slight refreshment in almost breathless silence, the general filled his glass with wine, and, turning to the officers, said, "With a heart full of love and gratitude I now take leave of you. I most devoutly wish that your latter days may be as prosperous and happy as your former ones have been glorious and honorable. I cannot come to each of you to take my leave, but shall be obliged if each one will come and take me by the hand." General Knox, being nearest to him, turned to the commander-in-chief, who, suffused, in tears, was incapable of utterance, but grasped his hand, when they embraced each other in silence. In the same affectionate manner every officer in the room marched up to, kissed, and parted with his General-in-Chief. Such a scene of sorrow and weeping I had never before witnessed, and I hope I may never be called upon to witness again. Not a word was uttered to break the solemn silence that presided or to interrupt the tenderness of the scene. The simple thought that we were about to part with the man who had conducted us through a long and bloody war, and under whose conduct the glory and independence of our country had been achieved, and that we should see his face no more in this world, seemed to be utterly insupportable. But the time of separation had come, and waving his hand to his grieving children around him, he left the room, and passing through a corps of light infantry who were paraded to receive him, he walked silently on to Whitehall, where a barge was waiting. We all followed in mournful silence to the wharf, where a prodigious crowd had assembled to witness the departure of the man, who, under God, had been the great agent in establishing the glory and independence of these United States. As soon as he was seated, the barge put off into the river, and when out in the stream, our great and beloved general waved his hat and bade us a silent adieu.

At Annapolis, where Congress was in session, Washington resigned his commission as commander-in-chief and left for Mount Vernon to resume his duties as a private citizen.

And the travail was over.

16 _Genesis_

AND there was a new nation. New not only in time but in kind. Yet those who lived within it hardly were aware of it, and there were still many who were hankering for the "good old days." Like the poor, the whiners of the past are always with us. Every exodus must have its desert where the old generation dies.

At this time New York, capital of the United States, had a population of a little more than ten thousand inhabitants; its treasury was empty, its trade ruined. There were no banks, no insurance offices, no charitable institutions, no open schools. Even the books and accounts of the Corporation had been carried off by a Mr. Cruger, treasurer and traitor, who had joined the British army and vanished.

But already New York showed its mettle and its genius. Within a decade its population trebled and its trade beat all her previous records. The great harbors of Europe hailed its boats, and it was already competing for China and the Far East with Boston and Salem.

The Hudson, so valuable during the War—with defenses at Fort Washington, Fort Lee, Stony Point, Verplanck's Point, Fort Independence, Fort Clinton, Fort Montgomery, Fort Arnold, Fort Putnam, Constitution Island, West Point, and fire-rafts anchored between Anthony's Nose and Bear Mountain—once again resumed its importance in peace. Once again it became the great artery between New York and Albany and, *via* the Great Lakes, to all points West and North and between New York and the rest of the Earth, which was so vast then, which has so shrunken now.

Long before the days of the transatlantic steamer you could see in the New York harbor the square-rigged ships, the schooners, the brigs that were going or returning from all the four corners of the world. Not to mention the packet ship, noted for its strength and speed and safety. The best of these would cross the Atlantic from New York to Liverpool in about two weeks, but in later years these good ships were abandoned for long trips.

The trips upon the Hudson were also for pleasure and health. You have but to take a trip some moonlit night from the Battery to Albany, and even if you have sailed over the Seine or the Danube or the Rhine, you will say: "My eyes are beholding loveliness." Or if you watch, from your apartment window on Riverside Drive or from a porch across the Jersey palisades, the boat sailing like a lighted altar and the fluted golden reflections in the water like pipes of a vast organ, you are caught with nostalgia and irresistible wanderlust.

Stage lines, too, connected New York with Albany, Boston and Philadelphia. Stages left twice a week, and three days were required to reach Albany in good summer weather but a few days more in the winter. And what the trip did to the posteriors may be surmised but is not recorded in the annals of stage-craft. Nor could a sleepyhead undertake such trips, for they started for Albany at five o'slock in the morning and for Boston at three, and the postilions whipped their horses until ten at night. Nor was the price something to be sneezed at—four pence a mile, which in modern coin should be at least a quarter of a dollar.

There was also the problem of trade regulations and duty

among the states, for it was a loose confederation as yet, and each state was jealous of its prerogatives and sovereignty. Retaliatory measures followed in quick succession and conditions began to take on a dark hue. The struggle for the adoption of the Federal Constitution was long and bitter. The Clinton faction, reflecting the manorial lords and the agricultural back country, preferred state autonomy while the Hamilton followers, workers and city people, desired a strong central government supporting commerce and providing a sound currency. This clash between the agricultural portion of the State and the large cities still continues, for other stakes naturally. The final vote was 30 to 27 for a Federal Government. On what small margins Ahura Mazda, the spirit of good overcomes Ahriman, the spirit of evil! And what sweat, blood, and tears must be stirred into the ammunition! New York was the eleventh state to sign the Constitution of the United States at Poughkeepsie, on July 26, 1788.

The first Federal Congress, seated in Federal Hall, formerly City Hall, in Wall Street, declared, after having canvased the returns from the electoral colleges, the unanimous election of George Washington as the first President of the United States. It took a week to inform Washington, and on the last day of April he was inaugurated, with pomp and majesty, President.

There was much rejoicing in the city and great bonfires, and Washington had to go home on foot, "the throng of people being so great as not to permit a carriage to pass through it."

Washington had his residence first at the corner of Cherry and Dover Streets, then at the Macomb mansion at 39 Broadway. John Adams, the vice president, lived in Richmond Hill. Thomas Jefferson, the Secretary of State, resided at what is now 57 Maiden Lane. Alexander Hamilton, the Secretary of

the Treasury, had his dwelling at 58 Wall Street. Henry
Knox, Secretary of War, resided in lower Broadway and had
a "garden running back to the river." Edmund Randolph,
Attorney-General, lived in the same street with the Knoxes.
John Jay, Chief Justice of the Supreme Court, dwelt at what
was then 133 Broadway.

On May 28 the President gave his first dinner, and the next
day Mrs. Washington held her first reception, "a simple and
unostentatious ceremony." But the ball in honor of Washington given by Comte de Moustier, the French ambassador,
was a different sort of affair.

After the President came, a company of eight couples formed in
the other room and entered, two by two, and began a most curious dance called En Ballet. Four of the gentlemen were dressed
in French regimentals, and four in American uniforms; four of
the ladies with blue ribbons round their heads and American
flowers, and four with red roses and flowers of France. These
danced in a very curious manner, sometimes two and two, sometimes four couple and four couple, and then in a moment all together, which formed great entertainment for the spectators, to
show the happy union between the two nations. Three rooms
were filled and the fourth was most elegantly set off as a place of
refreshment. A long table crossed this room from wall to wall.
The whole wall inside was covered with shelves filled with cakes,
oranges, apples, wines of all sorts, ice-cream, etc., and highly
lighted up. A number of servants from behind the table supplied
the guests with everything they wanted, from time to time, as
they came in to refresh themselves, which they did as soon as a
party had done dancing and made way for another. We retired
about ten o'clock, in the height of the jollity.

And Noah Webster, a New York editor at the time, writes:

In point of sociability and hospitality, New York is hardly ex-
celled by any town in the United States. The principal families

by associating in their public amusements with the middle-class
of well-bred citizens render their rank subservient to the happi-
ness of society, and prevent that party-spirit which an affectation
of superiority in certain families in Philadelphia has produced in
that city,—a spirit which disturbs or destroys their public amusements, and which has given the citizens, too generally perhaps,
the reputation of being inhospitable. . . .

And Webster adds: "The neatness, industry and parsimony
of the Dutch, were the characteristics of the citizens of New
York before the Revolution, and will probably be visible in
their manners long after national distinctions are lost."

In August 1790, New York ceased to be the capital of the
nation, and Mrs. Adams, the vice president's wife, despite
her diplomatic praises of the new capital, mourned the passing of the old. "When all is done, it will not be Broadway."

And in 1798 Albany became the state capital. New York
took the two events in its stride, as it had always done and
was further destined to do. As indeed, it had to do again that
very same year, for a terrible epidemic of yellow fever
scourged the city, killing hundreds upon hundreds and forcing all business to suspend. But out of the tragedy the New
York Hospital, which had been neglected and used as a barracks, took on a new life and became one of the great institutions of the city.

But even worse than this was the scourge of the new war.
The French Revolution had stirred the hearts and minds of
men, but a few years later, it was trampled upon by the little
Corporal from Corsica, and the motto of *Liberté* now became *Gloire,* and the world moaned and bled, for the sheen
of glory is the red of man's blood and the song of glory is
the cry of man's pain. England, still sore that she had lost
her colonies and in need of sailors, dared to invoke the right
of search of our vessels, and we retaliated by an embargo on

all vessels in American harbors; it was a double-edged sword that seemed to cut the throat of New York's commerce.

"Everything wore a dismal aspect at New York." There were bankruptcies by the dozen amounting to over five million dollars, and there were five hundred vessels rotting and thousands of sailors wandered about the country, paupers. Counting-houses shut down and clerks were dismissed, and farmers found no incentive to cultivate their lands, and sell their produce. And the national treasury received not a cent from the usual revenue, which on an average amounted to four and a half millions per year.

Later, when the English impudence had pushed us to a breaking point, and we declared war upon her, there was many a bold spirit in New York who, seeking revenge, joined the navy. Indeed, twenty-six privateers were fitted out at the port, carrying two hundred and twelve guns and over two thousand men.

How big and mighty the Atlantic was in those days, and yet could we hide from the battles that were taking place on the other side of its waters? Could we pull the great tides over us like a downy quilt and sleep in peace? The Little Corporal of Corsica strutted from Paris to Vienna, from Vienna to Moscow, and *we* felt the earth shake under us, and *we* had war, and the British set fire to the White House and the Capitol.

The nightmare which was Napoleon over, and our war with England terminated, we finally began to get into our stride. But not immediately. There were many odds and ends to be solved. The war had brought much confusion and commerce and industry. The government was nearly bankrupt. The former "aristocrats" were reluctant to accept the truth that "all men are created equal," even as the phony aristocrats of our own day try with pompous emptiness to give the words false and futile interpretations, until they seem the ridiculous concoction of mad utopians.

And how the great landowners shrieked when their estates were divided among those who actually tilled it and had worked upon it for generations. You might have thought their very arms and legs were amputated. One of these estates —the Van Rensselaer—up the Hudson was two-thirds the size of Rhode Island. And were not the heroes of two wars entitled to a bit of the land that they had freed? The rich graciously relinquish heaven to the poor, and oppressors believe in justice provided it is general, and not particular.

It was August 17, 1807, and crowds hurried to Greenwich Village dock to see *The Devil In A Sawmill,* otherwise known in history as the *Clermont,* a "monstrosity" invented by Fulton. This was not the first time that steam navigation had been experimented with. At the end of the seventeenth century there were already men who tried to put into use the new legs of man. Many were the names which preceded Fulton—Blasco de Gary, Papin, Jonathan Hulls, William Henry, Count d'Auxiron, M. Perier, Marquis de Jouffroy, James Rumsey, Nathan Reed, John Fitch—Englishmen and French and Spaniards and Italians.

The *Clermont* was one hundred and thirty feet long, sixteen feet wide, four feet deep, and had one hundred and sixty tons measurement. The engine had a steam cylinder twenty-four inches in diameter, with a four-foot stroke. The boiler was twenty by seven by eight, and the wheels measured fifteen feet in diameter. Her smoke stack was ridiculously tall and her paddle-wheels were uncovered. And she deserved, all in all, the appellation of "monstrosity." But what ingrate finds his mother ugly, and what magnificent modern liner should not devote one pulse of her electric heart to do honor to her incredible progenitor?

And what a day that was.

Nothing could exceed the surprise [wrote a contemporary], of all who witnessed the experiment. The minds of the most incredulous were changed in a few minutes. Before the boat had made the progress of a quarter of a mile, the greatest unbeliever must have been converted. The man, who, while he looked on the expensive machine, thanked his stars that he had more wisdom than to waste his money on such idle schemes, changed the expression of his features as the boat moved from the wharf and gained her speed; his complacent smile gradually stiffened into an expression of wonder. The jeers of the ignorant, who had neither sense nor feeling enough to suppress their contemptuous ridicule and rude jokes, were silenced for a moment by a vulgar astonishment, which deprived them of the power of utterance, till the triumph of genius extorted from the incredulous multitude which crowded the shores, shouts and acclamations of congratulation and applause.

And Robert Fulton wrote to the *American Citizen:*

I left New York on Monday at one o'clock, and arrived at Clermont, the seat of Chancellor Livingston, at one o'clock on Tuesday—time, twenty-four hours; distance, one hundred and ten miles. On Wednesday, I departed from the Chancellor's at nine in the morning, and arrived at Albany at five in the afternoon—distance forty miles; time, eight hours. The sum is one hundred and fifty miles in thirty-two hours, equal to near five miles an hour. . . . Throughout my whole way, both going and returning, the wind was ahead; no advantage could be derived from my sails: the whole has, therefore, been performed by the power of the steam-engine.

I am, sir, your obedient servant,

Robert Fulton.

The *Clermont* was followed by scores of other boats, barbaric in gorgeous display of gingerbread and gold, and yet:

Those great, resplendent, costly, comfortless, tasteless vessels, overloaded with ornament and magnificently vulgar, were the pride of the towns from which they hailed, and each boat had its retinue of eager partisans, always ready to engage in a wordy warfare concerning the respective merits of their favorite and their rivals.

And as late as 1840, N. P. Willis writes:

Just off from the wharf, with a freight of seven or eight hundred souls hoping to "take tea" in Albany. The scene is one of inextricable confusion, and it is not till the twenty miles of the Palisades are well passed that the bewildered passenger knows rightly whether his wife, child, or baggage, whichever may be his tender care, is not being left behind at the rate of fifteen miles an hour. . . . By this time the young ladies are tired of looking at the Palisades, and have taken out their novels, the old gentlemen are poring over their damp newspapers, and the captain has received his fourteen hundred or two thousand dollars, locked up his office, and gone to smoke with the black funnel and the engineer.

The Great River found the new vehicles no burden. Its back is strong, its legs planted securely in beds of rock that challenged all the hammers of time. But time now was in a hurry, and it outflanked the waters of the River. Time invented the railroad and the automobile and the airplane and the telephone and the radio. The River flowed on, but it was no longer the great bringer of goods and the bringer of news and the teller of heroic tales of battle and of romance. Its great ramparts, the Palisades, were worn off almost to the gums like a hag's teeth by shovels and drills, and across, on the Manhattan side, the rocks were carried off and the paths flattened. Only plaques here and there nailed into walls or cemented into pedestals now remind their casual readers that those are spots sacred to history. Alas, that the gods of one generation should become the worm-eaten statues of the next and that the entire bulk of the past should be out-weighed by each ephemeral instant of the present!

There are still vessels that cleave the Hudson's flanks—snub-nosed ferries that ply between the two shores; ships with fictitious smokestacks that travel overnight between the Battery and Albany during the summer, tugboats, fishing craft, rowboats, canoes. And during World War II, wounded merchant ships in dry dock, or assembled to slip away in convoys in the dead of night; and, in victory, great battle wagons anchored for Presidential inspection.

No doubt that the Grande Rivière is still useful, as an ancient member of the family may still earn her bread and board by doing a light chore or watch over the latest infant while the parents are out on pleasure or at work. But its destiny has already been fulfilled—the creation of a great new world.

THE HUDSON

'Twas a vision of childhood that came with its dawn,
Ere the curtain that covered life's day-star was drawn;
The nurse told the tale when the shadows grew long,
And the mother's soft lullaby breathed it in song.

"There flows a fair stream by the hills of the west,"—
She sang to her boy as he lay on her breast;
"Along its smooth margin their fathers have played;
Beside its deep waters their ashes are laid."

I wandered afar from the land of my birth,
I saw the old rivers, renowned upon earth,
But fancy still painted that wide-flowing stream
With the many-hued pencil of infancy's dream.

I saw the green banks of the castle-crowned Rhine,
Where the grapes drink the moonlight and change it to wine;
I stood by the Avon, whose waves as they glide
Still whisper his glory who sleeps at their side.

But my heart would still yearn for the sound of the waves
That sing as they flow by my forefathers' graves;
If manhood yet honors my cheek with a tear,
I care not who sees it,—no blush for it here.

Farewell to the deep-bosomed stream of the West.
I fling this loose blossom to float on its breast;
Nor let the dear love of its children grow cold,
Till the channel is dry where its waters have rolled.

—OLIVER WENDELL HOLMES

17 Highways and Byways

WE grew vertiginously, noisily, boastingly, joyfully, fearless of fate and man. We challenged with reckless bravado the ancient and cynical world, proclaiming: "These shores have neither gates nor walls nor fences. Let your outcasts come to us and be of us!" And the hungry and the hounded, the rebels and the dreamers, the restless young and the spirited old, from famous lands and lands uncharted, praying in a hundred fashions and speaking a thousand tongues—one million—ten million—twenty million—generation after generation—came. And their fears and their hunger, their hopes and their dreams, and the long memory of weary wandering were water and wind and sun, and the nation blossomed and was great, and its life was the breath of life to the burdened and the scourged of the Earth.

And already in 1835 the population of New York city was two hundred thousand. Duties collected in one year were above ten million dollars. There were fifteen hundred mercantile houses, twelve banks, ten marine insurance companies. There were schools and newspapers and magazines—and graft and corruption.

But other cities were growing and prospering and claiming attention, and it would not be so long now before New York would be the Empire State. A frontier period, a miniature covered-wagon exodus, preceded and followed the turn of the nineteenth century. The forests were cleared,

168

houses erected, land plowed, schools and colleges established, and the population of the State had reached nearly a million and a half by 1820. It was the first among the sister states.

By 1850 New York State possessed one-seventh of the true valuation of the property of the whole country. By 1850, also, it had given the nation two presidents, five vice presidents, and many cabinet officers.

The Erie Canal, the 363-mile "ditch," was finally completed at a cost of seven million dollars in 1825. So successful was this that ten branch canals were constructed. Through the great reduction in freight rates and the improved accessibility of markets and supplies, the canal system provided a tremendous stimulus to settlement and development in agriculture, commerce, and industry. Buffalo became the eastern terminal for the Lakes trade and New York the Nation's major port—the Nation's and eventually the World's.

Soon another factor was to revolutionize the State's transportation—the railroad. At first it was considered an auxiliary to waterways and kept in that secondary position because of the State's canal investments. By 1851, however, it was becoming quite evident that this artificial condition could no longer continue, and the railroad took its rightful place in the State's circulatory system.

The history of the building and owning of the railroads rivals that of the Borgias; it tells such names as Daniel Drew, James Fisk, Jay Gould, Cornelius Vanderbilt—but we are not here interested in exposing the lust of gold (and the lust of power which is even more terrifying).

In the 30's there were several small lines crossing the State, but in 1853 all of them were consolidated to form the New York Central. Similarly, other lines gathered into the Delaware and Hudson, and the Erie. At present there are ten systems operating nearly ten thousand miles of track.

Men of New York State contributed greatly to the further-
ance of the railways. At the very inception of this means of
locomotion, scouts on horseback located trains and brake-
men by sheer physical force stopped them.

The telegraph was first used by the New York railroads,
and Wells and Fargo were among the earliest express companies. George Westinghouse of New York invented the air
brake, and Woodruff of Watertown and Wagner of the Palatine Bridge introduced the first sleeping cars, and in 1890
the Pullman Palace Car Company was organized.

A tributary, so to say, to the great river of steel, was the
street car. It flowed in all directions, united suburbs, gave
impetus to growth of cities, encouraged the opening of picnic
and amusement parks. And since man never forgets love, the
"Twilight Trolley Tour" was especially run over 25-mile net-
works for lovesick couples. These cars were decorated with
colored lights, appropriately dimmed, for after all that was
the age of spooning, not of necking, of long engagements, not
instantaneous wedlock.

The history of the street car is finished, tracks lifted, wires
cut, bells forever silenced, its place being taken by the bus,
which in turn will be supplanted by what? Yet here and
there, on the road, the old-timer recognizes a car, now transformed into a lunch-wagon, and there is a tug at his heart,
for who knows but he might have ridden in it, holding hands
with what phantom maid, who, doubtless, is also transformed
from a winged being to something staid and without dreams.
As for himself, he'd better enter the wagon, order his ham-
burger, and forget.

The bicycle appeared as "the devil on wheels" (all new
ideas, new ways, new delights, as well as the ancient pleasure of pleasures being ascribed to that inventive genius) at
about the same time. It started as a craze. Organized into

clubs, the cyclists built and maintained hundreds of miles of
cinder paths. They were the *leit motif* of innumerable songs,
jests, and parodies, not to mention sermons, directed particularly against the ladies and their bloomers. And the smoke
rising from the mountains of female flesh cast into the fires of
hell by preachers and near-preachers must have indeed
pleased the nostrils of his Satanic Majesty.

With the appearance of the automobile, the bicycle was
relegated to a toy fit for youngsters and at a point almost
disappeared like some unessential fifth wheel of locomotion.
During World War II, however, the bicycle had a temporary
resurrection.

And then came the automobile. Inauspicious and ridiculous was its infancy. What middle-aged, pot-bellied, bald, or
grayish man does not remember shouting after the "gas buggies" as a boy, "Git a horse! Git a horse!"? And who, of the
younger set, has not seen in the movies queerly dressed
people—attempting to set in motion something that snorted
and pawed and vomited smoke, but were constrained at last
to have recourse to that noble beast, himself almost forgotten
now—*equus caballus*—whose essence is in the lovely word,
"chivalry"?

Quickly was the infancy over, and the adolescence, and
before you knew it that "crazy" piece of machinery changed
the face of the State, the temper of the people, the meaning
of home. We became nomads, but also explorers. We had no
time to meditate, but our eyes saw what our minds had not
perceived. The peasant turned gentleman farmer and the
small-towner a cosmopolitan, while the city man and his
children became acquainted with forest and mountain and
cow and cowslip. And of course, the envious and impotent,
in the role of shocked mentors, shouted: "Our morals—our
morals are dead!" And they blamed the illegitimate descend-

ants upon the "brothels on wheels," forgetting haystacks and grassy knolls and all the accommodating furniture throughout the centuries and the lands.

The speed with which the automobile became the revolutionizer of our life was largely due to a man of unrelieved mediocrity—Henry Ford—who had a small merchant's intuition for underselling his competitors. He came on time and therefore he appeared a genius. And his billion-dollar profit has been as a vast pedestal on which totters a tiny statue. But there are those, who for one reason or another, in the measure of the man include the statue.

O tempora. O mores. Who would laugh now at the magnificent streamlined vehicles which dash by and so often run us over—hundreds of thousands each year throughout the nation—tribute to this new Moloch in all the hundreds of valleys of Tophet. And our State (without boasting) has its proportionate number of victims. But is it Moloch or Madness? Death is ambushed between one breath and another. It is safer to go to war than to cross the highways. The machine obeys. Is it the fault of the machine if the one it is constrained to obey is a fool, a scoundrel, a youth drunken with youth or an adult drunken with spirits?

At the beginning of World War II there were close to three million motor vehicles registered in the State and more than one-seventh of the workers in the nation were directly or indirectly engaged in the automotive industry.

The highways now became motorways, and engineering had to be revised and relearned, and licensing and regulation of traffic became a state concern. No private enterprise could cope with the countless ramifications. From 1922 to the end of 1935 the State appropriated nearly $6 billion for its highways, in addition to the Federal grants amounting to $128 million. A five-year plan was then adopted calling for further improvements to conform to the needs of modern traffic.

Meanwhile, bridges had to be built, and some of them are a splendid combination of art and engineering, and many counties devised three- and four-lane boulevards through landscaped parkways, such as those in Westchester and Long Island, for example.

Man watched the bird and was jealous. He could walk and run as other animals; he could crawl on his belly like the snake (and with as much venom in him) in the presence of his lords; he could swim like the fish; he could jump like the kangaroo; but he could not fly. A tiny bit of life, the weight of his thumb, could twit him from the topmost branch of a tree.

Wings have always been on the agenda of man. He created angels, implanted wings on Mercury's heels and on the back of the most famous and the most capricious of all stallions, Pegasus. If only he could push his head into the clouds. Leonardo Da Vinci tried his hand at the balloon and nearly succeeded in being burned at the stake, for there were those in power who feared man might see what goes on behind the clouds, which they used as an "iron curtain" for their interests.

But man is obstinate. He went on trying. As early as 1670 artificial wings were used, but of all things artificial, wings are the least secure. In 1783 the first balloon of modern times made its appearance and remained in the air. Thereafter, until the construction of the biplane of the Wright brothers, the balloon was the only successful device for navigating the upper sea.

The rest every schoolboy knows as well as the hundreds of millions living in the vast ruins which once were great cities. So far man-with-wings has been a vulture to man.

The Empire State, naturally, has taken a leading part in the development and use of the airplane, and Idlewild and La Guardia Field in New York City are two of the largest and best equipped in the nation, and more than a hundred others are recognized by the Bureau of Air Commerce. American airlines maintain regular schedules in the principal cities. Whether the State can keep its supremacy in the air, or New York City its world pre-eminence, is in the laps of the gods. The plane will surely change the meaning of geography and may bestow its favors upon what are now humbler spots. Every history is the recital not alone of the rise but also the fall of men, as of nations.

Since we have spoken of turnpikes and railroads, of street cars and automobiles, of boats and planes, it may seem that we have exhausted the means of transportation in our State, but there are subtler ones, not generally considered as such —the telephone, the telegraph, and, in particular, the radio and television. In the hold of the word more things are carried than in all the vehicles ever devised by man—and the cargo is more precious and more perilous. In the beginning was the Word—and in the end, also, the Word.

And so we stretched and pushed in all directions, as a youth will—whether he is tree or man or state, and we made room for our ideas and our goods. The post-Civil War period saw the urbanization and industrialization of the State in geometric progression. And the crown rested more securely upon the Empire State.

18 What Man Lives By

MAN talks big. He says "I and the Cosmos," "I and Nature." He stands on a little hill and crows to all the suns to shine or set, but the barnyard cock is as successful. The truth is that man tears himself away from his mother but there is no knife sharp enough to cut the umbilical cord that unites him to Earth. Indeed, if the grasses of Earth had not for millions of years before man's advent stored up that priceless green material, chlorophyll, he and all his colleagues, the mammals, would never have lived to trample upon them and devour them.

Some jealous neighbor said: "New York has everything." And it has. The name conjures visions of great cities and canyons of steel and stone, but New York is even in farm products near the top of the list—the seventh, to be precise, among its sister states. It leads in cabbage, milk, and onions. It is the second in potatoes, apples, hay, cherries, beets; third in eggs, carrots, and lettuce, fourth in pears and celery. And in buckwheat and honey, it stands supreme.

Do you desire precise figures to convince you? New York's total yearly production of corn, wheat, barley, oats, rye, and buckwheat in 1955 was 60 million bushels, while in canning, it wavered between first and second among its competitors, with a gross business of over $100 million. There are 125,000 farms totaling 15 million acres. The livestock has a value of over $200 million. To round off the matter, the farm population is 600,000.

The history of agriculture in New York is not of recent date nor of one artificially stimulated. During the Revolution the Empire State had the honor of being called "the granary of the Revolution," in somewhat the same sense as during the war our nation was known as "the arsenal of democracy." The soil, the climate, and the improved means of transportation, each contributed to establish the State as essentially agricultural. With the exception of some of the rock regions among the mountains and a few sandy hills, the State is highly cultivable. In the River Valley the soil is composed largely of alluvium, but that in the uplands is formed from decomposed limestone, shale, and native rock, adaptable for growing farm crops, fruits, and vegetables. The climate, too, is friendly. Rare, until the last few years, were the tumultuous upheavals—the hurricane, the floods, the snowbound winters, and the annual rainfall, as an average, is about thirty-five inches in most of the State.

Poultry raising, the second source of the State's agricultural income, is largely concentrated on Long Island. Each year near to 25 million chickens are raised and the eggs these creatures graciously offer run into billions, while their quacking cousins, the "Long Island ducklings," have joined the ranks of the fowl aristocracy.

If you have a sweet tooth, you will envisage with pleasure the cataract of syrup produced from the maple sugar—500,000 gallons per season, plus 500,000 pounds of sugar. And if you believe that an apple a day keeps the doctor away, you will have great cause to rejoice, for no other State in the Union, except Washington, has an apple crop equal to our own—eight million trees and 20 million bushels.

But you may prefer peaches. The State produces two mil-

lion bushels of the fuzzy-faced a year. Or is it pears, perhaps?
The pear, once the jewel of its family, as late as 1870 sold
for a dollar apiece. Still as sweet, but no longer as ritzy, it
fills over 500,000 bushels each twelvemonth. And the deco-
rative cherry, dangling so merrily from lovely ears, rises to
a mountain of 37,000 tons. And the grape?

> How long, how long, in infinite pursuit
> Of this and that endeavour and dispute?
> Better be merry with the fruitful grape
> Than sadden after none, or bitter, fruit.

Over 88,000 tons. And wineries produce not only still
wines but the "fermented-in-the-bottle." Shall we ever rival
the French in champagne? Do we wish to? Have we the
heart to destroy romance and tradition?

The New York Farmers have learned how to protect themselves. There are Dairymen's Leagues and Co-operative
Grange Leagues, which have thousands of members and do
several hundred million dollars' worth of business yearly.

The State, too, has within recent years held out a helping
hand to the farmers, but it remains true now and for all
time that God helps him who helps himself. Still, the State
of New York has done a great service with the establishment
of the State College of Agriculture at Cornell University, its
experiment station at Geneva, and six other State schools of
agriculture. Here the coming generations of farmers will
learn the principles and practices of scientific farming. To
these we may add the special radio programs for farmers
and pamphlets dealing with a wide variety of problems, such
as conservation by crop rotation, the use of fertilizer, and the
acquisition of submarginal land.

The county fair has been for a century and a half an excellent meeting ground for farmers and, in a sense, the first

college of agriculture, for through jealousy, admiration, or cupidity, the participants learned new and better ways. The State, cognizant of the importance of fairs, subsidizes them in part.

The Department of Agriculture has fifteen bureaus at present, with its headquarters at Albany and branch offices in other principal cities of the State.

And the day may yet come when the swords shall be beaten into ploughs, and the ploughman shall receive his due of honor and comfort and security. And the weather, too, shall cease its age-long enmity and, placing its head under the yoke of science, shall become man's good and predictable friend.

Industrially, New York is self-made. Neither the Dutch nor the English gave it the appropriate push. The Dutch were chiefly fur traders intent upon cheating the Indians by giving them cheap cloth, hatchets, guns, and liquor for valuable beaver. Even the craftsmen sent over by the Dutch patroons deserted their trades and engaged in the black market.

The exit of the Dutch and the entrance of the British partly changed matters. The fur trade declined somewhat, but the State remained agricultural. With the manorial system established, the quasi-medieval existence was in full swing. Moreover, the mercantile policy of Great Britain prohibited the manufacture of all goods except household necessities. Every manor was self-sufficient. The women made the cloth for the family, itinerant weavers wove it, and the local mill finished it. Shoes were made from home-tanned leather. Clay for brick was puddled by the tread of horses. The goods sold in stores, however, had to be brought from the "mother" country. We were a colony created in the image of greed for

the good and the glory and the greatness of the Crown and
those upon whom it cast its rays.

For a half-century after the Revolution Britain continued
to forbid the export of machinery to the new Nation, and
persisted in dumping its manufactured products upon the
American market. Only after the War of 1812, steadier on
our feet as an independent nation, we erected a protective
tariff and prevented the "mother" from forcing her goods
upon us. And so we started at last.

As the population began to spread in all directions, factory
products were in constant and growing demand. Still, up to
1830, although the volume increased there was little variety.
But as a child seems to shoot up overnight and become a
full-fledged youth, so did our State. Cloth, woolen and cotton
goods, glass, hardware appeared on the market. Then came
potash, nails, starch, paper, tobacco, chocolate, and snuff.

The 40's, spurred by the invention of the sewing machine,
brought the revolutionization of the clothing industry. No
longer did man have to wear one suit the greater part of his
life-time, then turn it on the other side, and finally bequeath
it to his first born, or woman depend upon her bridal trous-
seau for her attire as a grandmother. New York State, and
in particular New York City and Rochester, liberated the
world from rags. And the time was to come when a salesgirl
in a department store or a stenographer could vie with a lady
of high degree in fineries and with Cinderella in footwear.

By the middle of the century the State manufactured agricultural implements, furniture, hardware, silverware. There
were breweries and boatyards and factories for mirrors and
millstones, for soap and candles. Indeed, New York had definitely achieved its rank as the Empire State in industry.

The Civil War stimulated improvement and expansion in
all directions, as World Wars I and II were to do a few gen-

erations later. The blood of youth and the tears of age seem
to be an excellent fertilizer.

The largest industry in the State is still the manufacturing
of clothing and accessories, amounting to $2 billion yearly.
Rochester and Birmingham manufacture shoes; Poughkeepsie, Beacon, and Kingston hats and caps; and New York City
men's and women's clothes. In New York City alone there
are one thousand textile plants.

Other mammoth industries are printing and publishing,
amounting to a billion dollars annually; food $350 million in
flour and grain; and ice cream and confectionery, $100 mil-
lion. Less colossal, yet still quite respectable, are the manufacture of copper products, carpets, rugs, pottery, tile, and
porcelain, and Hudson Valley is the largest producer of common brick in the world. Are there workers among these
brickmakers who understand and sympathize with those who
made bricks without straw for the taskmasters of Pharaoh?

The newer industries based on modern scientific and tech-
nological studies are more than commonly represented. The
General Electric Company in Schenectady manufactures
heavy generating machinery, radio apparatus, refrigerators,
and induction motors, while Buffalo and Niagara Falls produce chemicals, dyes, abrasives, and metal alloys, and ultra
modern Buffalo has its grounds stampeded not by the wild
bulls but by airplanes and parachutes.

But what is all this steel, this fluid, this gas; what are all
these springs, these wires, these motors; what, indeed, is
everything you eat, you wear, the house you live in, the
plane you fly in, the radio you listen to—what, if not human
sweat, and often human blood, leavened by human tears?
Remove these, and you have removed the soul, the spirit,
the breath. You may still have, as on a dissecting table, or-
gans to be weighed and labeled—but where is life?

Where did these people come from who gave their sweat and blood and tears to make the State of New York the Empire State? They came from every part of the Earth. How were they treated by the older inhabitants? Regretfully, we must repeat the Latin proverb, borrowed from the Greeks, borrowed from the first ancients who looked at the world and sighed—*homo homini lupus,* "man is wolf to man." And to continue the jungle illustration, the leopard came to the new habitat but he kept his spots. For the immigrants brought the good and the evil of their former homes and planted them in the New World, and the fruits of the trees were the same, honeyed or filled with ashes, as they had been in the Old World. Yet gradually there appeared a new variety with a different tang and different perfume.

After the Revolution the people of the State began to breathe more freely, and the workers, who had united to fight the enemy from beyond the ocean, now united to fight the enemy who despoiled them and exploited them in their own home. Already in 1800 we find the cyclical pattern: organization and protest, collective action, and political pressure; then inertia and stagnation, and once again new leaders and a resurgence of activity.

In 1829 the "Workies" organized in New York City (where the initiative was always taken), and the movement spread in the conservative upstate. The issues were the 10-hour day, free education for all, abolition of imprisonment for debt. While the party achieved a modicum of its platform, it split on religious and racial questions—ancient and terrible diseases.

Then came the Utopian experiments of Fourierism and the Oneida Community, and only after the middle of the nineteenth century did the unions emerge strongly and continue to gain ground. The New York Printers' Union, formed in

1850, became the International Typographical Union in 1869. Trades Assemblies were formed in industrial centers. Craft unionism blossomed into The American Federation of Labor, led by Samuel Gompers. Socialism reached its peak under the leadership of Eugene Debs, and was supplanted by Communism, and the gigantic battle of ideologies is now in progress.

19 Education and Sundry Matters

IS education learning or unlearning? Often it is more difficult to scrape off the barnacles of lies that cling to an old
truth than to discover a new one. And education, if rightly
presented and rightly pursued, should be a knife to do the
paring. But in wrong hands it may cut the heart of the truth
and leave the barnacles intact. It may do worse still. It may
carve the barnacles into objects of admiration and worship.
No scoundrel is as dangerous as the educated scoundrel.

At the head of the New York State educational system is
the Board of Regents with the Commissioner of Education
as its chief executive. The Board is composed of twelve
members elected for twelve years. It charters colleges and
universities and associations for the promotion of education.
It has a voice in budgeting the State-supported colleges of
agriculture, veterinary medicine, and home economics. It has
complete jurisdiction over the State's teachers' colleges and
normal schools. It prescribes regulations for admission to
professional schools and syllabi and examinations for high
schools. It confers honorary degrees.

The "little red schoolhouse" was first established in 1812,
but it was only after the Civil War that the great common
school system was firmly rooted. There are now over eleven
thousand elementary schools, fourteen hundred high schools,
sixteen schools for defectives and delinquents, and twenty-
two Indian schools on reservations. The student body in-

cludes nearly two and a half million in the elementary and over a million in the high schools. Private and parochial schools count 650 thousand. The State of New York spends over one million dollars a day on education.

But you may wish to know the names of some of our famous institutions of learning, and their ages. Here they are: Columbia University, 1754; Union College, 1795 (before the Civil War it was the largest college in the nation); Hamilton College, 1812; Hobart, 1825; the oldest engineering school, Rensselaer Polytechnic Institute, 1826. (To understand what a little more than a century has done to the meaning and objectives of education, ponder over the apologetic tone of the charter granted to the above institution: "For the purpose of instructing persons who may choose to apply themselves in the application of science to the common purposes of life.") Colgate (formerly Madison), 1846; Rochester, 1851; Cornell, 1865; Syracuse, 1870; Elmira, the first to be devoted to the education of women, 1855; followed by Vassar, 1861; and Wells, 1868. In New York City, besides Columbia and Barnard, its women's branch, we have New York University (formerly University of the City of New York), 1831, and under its present name since 1896. Fordham University (Catholic, originally St. John's College), 1841; Cooper Union, 1859; the City-owned colleges Hunter, Brooklyn, Queens, and City College, the last named dates from 1847, the others are more recent additions.

Never in time and space has there been so much machinery for educating a people—and in many ways such excellent machinery. Never, generally speaking, such well-trained pedagogues. Never so many years allowed a child to wander in the halls of knowledge. Well, are we getting educated, or aren't we? Are we preparing Adam of New York to live in an atom world? Shall we prepare him to live for the present or for the future? And shall he ignore or forget the past? Shall the emphasis be good citizenship, intelligence, culture? Or, are they all the same thing? Shall we allow propaganda in the classroom, or is propaganda the death of democracy? Shall we teach facts or thinking? But facts are only bricks— and only what we build with them counts. As for thinking, much of the mental gymnastics taught have no more relation to thinking than vertigo has to dancing. Shall it be truth? Can man stomach truth undiluted with illusions, whatever their pompous names may be? Leave truth to the meta- physicians and teach us the truths. But every truth is a small oasis in the vast desert of ignorance and perennially in danger of being swallowed up by the sandstorms. Shall we have expert but uncultured specialists, or cultured and less expert specialists? Let us have the expert *and* cultured. But there is no time. Life is short and science is long.

What about character? Do our schools teach character? What is character? An impression—an engraving—a brand— a stamp? Is one born with it? Is it acquired? Environment or heredity? The family has the child for the first six or seven years of his life—is he lost to education thereafter? Are most of the monstrous prejudices forever carved into his brain and heart while still in his trundle bed by those whose inter- est it is that he never grow up mentally?

How about juvenile delinquency? Is the school the pivotal cause? Or the parents? Or society? Is it economics? Are the poor more criminal than the rich?

Oh, the grandiose tournaments between the valiant knights —Tradition and Iconoclasm. What clashes of armor! What hills of broken lances! What forests of paper consumed! What cataracts of ink! What whirlwinds of winds! Oh, the cannonades of statistics! Oh, the thunderclaps of generalities!

And even if Fang Tu, the great poet of China, be right in

his poem, entitled "Fang Tu Explains to a Bookworm the
Futility of Knowledge":

> Mass shadow upon black shadow,
> O learned Tai,
> Shall they ever rise,
> Majestic,
> Like the Tall Mountain
> That watches
> The round waters
> Of the Yellow Lake?
> Shall they ever press
> More heavily
> Earth's patient face
> Than the ruffled feather
> A fledgling drops?

Even if he be right—blessed is the State in which people
quarrel about the meaning of truth and the purpose of education and the great values of culture. Their words are jets
of light. They are keys to treasures. They are hammers crushing chains.

People stop going to school and many stop reading books,
but who can live in our State without reading newspapers,
even if only the comics, which are becoming more and more
the favorite pabulum (or, according to the educators, the
favorite poison) of young and old?

After Civil War there was a blossoming of journalism. The
telegraph, the Associated Press, the stereotyping gave it a
tremendous boost. The weeklies became dailies and increased
their number of pages, and Sunday editions appeared for the
first time. The modern newspaper gradually emerged with
its miraculous news coverage, but also with its dangerous
standardization of editorials and feature articles. And here
are some of the newspapers: *The New York Times, The*

Herald Tribune, descendants of the papers of Horace Greeley
and James Gordon Bryant; The *Journal-American,* Hearst's
baby; The *Post,* whose great editor was William Cullen Bryant; The *Daily News,* having, alas, the largest circulation;
The *Daily Worker,* the Communist organ—all published in
New York. *Times-Union,* Albany; *Journal-News,* Ithaca;
Times-Union, Rochester; *Observer-Dispatch,* Utica.

In all, New York State has over two hundred dailies, one
thousand weeklies, thirty-five foreign language dailies, with
twenty-one Sunday editions.

Many magazines have their home offices in our State and
principally in New York City. Are they good? Are they bad?
Who shall be a judge of taste? Anyway, only they are right
who agree with us, but they who disagree with us find others
to agree with them, and thus it would seem that at any given
moment all mankind is right. The main point is that they are
freely published.

And hats off to our public libraries—best in the world. And
to our librarians, underpaid, overworked, patient, and ever
at your service, salute!

Who shall be called a New York writer—one who was born
in New York, one who lives in New York, one who writes
about New York? But all roads lead to New York (City) for
writers, as all roads once led to Rome for those who sought
power, fame, or trouble and the stake. We shall not mention
any living ones by name, for the sake of safety and impar-
tiality, for no grave is so forsaken as an artist ignored.

Literary history in New York State properly begins with
Washington Irving, for those who preceded him were either
slavish imitators of the English, or were of no consequence,
or both. Moreover, Irving was born in New York, wrote
about New York, lived in New York (except for his sojourn
in Europe), and died in New York. And what he wrote had

enduring quality. About the same period we have James Fenimore Cooper, who created the Indian in the image of the "unspoiled child of nature" and influenced, among others, French men of letters who, smothered by the perfume of boudoirs, gasped for a bit of fresh air.

Let us resurrect a few more—James K. Paulding and John H. Payne, collaborators with Irving; Joseph R. Drake; Fitz-Greene Halleck; Susan and Warner with best sellers; Nathaniel Parker Willis; John Burroughs, who loved his birds and trees and flowers as much as St. Francis loved them, but who knew them much better and who also created a few new ones; John T. Trowbridge; Frank G. Patchin, who wrote two hundred books of adventure for boys and girls; Edward Payson Roe, preacher turned author but still remained preacher, whose novels sold into the hundreds of thousands; Isabelle McDonald Alden, who wrote 120 volumes and sold phenomenally; Lyman Frank Baum, author of Wizard of Oz stories; Joseph Billings, humorist; Bret Harte, born, if not raised, in New York; Robert W. Chambers.

And two giants—Herman Melville, author of *Moby Dick,* one of the great American novels, neglected, misunderstood even by his friend Nathaniel Hawthorne, to whom he had given his heart and soul. And Walt Whitman, teacher, carpenter, editor, nurse, lover of democracy and of man, poet with few peers. Paralyzed, he sat upon his haunches in the small city of Camden, New Jersey, watching his puritanic critics pass him by into oblivion while his name became more and more synonymous with America. And with him, although not a New Yorker, lived and worked another poet and mighty lover of man, Horace Traubel, undeservedly forgotten.

Whoever says "theater" says New York City. For a century now the rest of the State, and indeed of the Union, has relinquished prerogative and judgment to Broadway, and more than once has rued the day, but so far it seems irrevocable. To classify actors or playwrights as New Yorkers merely by the accident of birth would reveal nothing of the significance of the stage, its glory and its misery, but we shall mention one name—Eugene O'Neill.

The theaters are many and beautiful and their doors are open to those who care to enter and have the required money, but those who wish their plays produced must first eat their own hearts.

The radio and television need no introduction, and New York has entered most of the homes of the world, the guest who remains not beyond his welcome. There are eighteen broadcasting stations and six television stations.

New York is the Mecca of music. Here the aspirants to fame and riches come to worship—and to die. No crown is valid until New York sets its seal upon it. Even as early as the 1770's there were musical societies in New York City, and Rochester had a brass band in 1817. The Maennerchoir was organized in 1854, the Rochester Philharmonic Society in 1865. In 1850 Jenny Lind sang in Albany. In 1842 the Philharmonic Society came into being, and the Metropolitan Opera House in 1883, and the world has not heard such music since Orpheus played on his golden lyre and enchanted gods and men and beasts and trees.

Man, fearful of the finality of death, as soon as his hand could hold a stone began to carve his image into it—and art began. Henri Couturier, a Frenchman, and four Duyckincks of three generations, were the first to paint Dutch New York. Evert Duyckinck, who settled in Long Island in 1683, painted the portraits of Van Cortlandt and other notables, while the Colonial families were painted by Robert Feke, born in 1705 on Long Island.

Benjamin West and John Trumbull depicted historical events after the Revolution and made portraits of the leaders. Robert Fulton and Samuel F. B. Morse, known for other things, also painted landscapes and portraits which have interested modern critics. Let us mention, too, Malbone for his delicate miniatures and Henry Inman for his genre subjects. The Hudson Valley and the Catskills aroused the admiration and attention of many of the artists, and in particular George Inness, John Kensett, and Frederick E. Church.

But we must hurry to meet James A. M. Whistler who, although he preferred Europe, was an undeniable son of New York, and John Lafarge, the father of American mural painting, and Augustus S. Gaudens, the sculptor, and Robert Henri who with his disciples formed the "New York Realists."

And what of architecture? For many generations New York was what the mother countries were—*new* Holland, *new* England, *new* France—and examples of the buildings are still extant, some charming and beautiful, others interesting only in the way our grandparents are interesting—that such magnificent blossoms as ourselves should have had such peculiar roots.

It took a long time for the American architect to wean himself from the Old World, but conditions forced him to change his ways. New structural systems, new building types, and new planning methods led to a new aesthetic approach. Whether you like what he has achieved is another matter again. The layman hopes that the future will bring him houses which will delight his eye and comfort his body. What the present offers him, he feels, is only transitional.

But what is education, art, culture, if the heart is stone? Already, during the Dutch administration, we find alms-

houses for the dependent aged and orphanmasters appointed
to take care of the propertied widows and orphans. The
Duke's Law in 1665, during the English rule, made each
parish responsible for its poor. But there was little "heart"
in all this. Poverty and its attendant misfortunes were divine
visitations caused by secret or open sin, and the attitude toward the sufferers was cold and straitlaced, and in many
places the pauper wore a brightly colored badge on his
sleeve inscribed with a large *P*.

After the Revolution we find a little warming of the human
blood. Corporal punishment gradually began to be abolished,
poor relief was secularized, and in 1824 the State legislature
passed "An Act to provide for the establishment of county
almshouses." In that same year the first House of Refuge for
Juvenile Delinquents was established.

The mentally ill, from time immemorial regarded with
terror and hate as linked to the powers of evil, were beginning to get a bit of mercy, and in 1834 the first municipal
mental hospital in this country, now the Manhattan State
Hospital, was founded. In 1865 the State Institution for the
Blind was established at Batavia.

And so, step by weary step, the people of the Empire State
abandoned the idea that misfortune and pain was the penalty of divinity and must be compounded with the cruelty
of man. Nor would they subscribe any longer to the notion
that the poor we must always have with us, that poverty,
indeed, was the natural and inevitable concomitant of
wealth. In June 1934 President Franklin D. Roosevelt created a committee on economic security, which set the basis
of the Social Security Act which became law in 1935. The
State of New York even broadened and deepened the scope
of social welfare. Provision was authorized

for the aid, care and support of the needy directly or through sub-
divisions of the State; or for the protection by insurance or otherwise, against the hazards of unemployment, sickness and old age;
or the education and support of the blind, the deaf, the dumb,
the physically handicapped and juvenile delinquents; or for the
health and welfare services for all children; or for the aid, care
and support of neglected and dependent children and of the
needy sick.

Let charity abide with us, but greater than charity is understanding, and the greatest of them all is justice.

A State lives not only by its realities but by its legends.
Legend is to history what the idiom is to language. It gives
flavor and personality. Our ancestors are shrewd prestidigi-
tators. They laugh at coffins. As soon as we turn our backs,
they come out. And there they are—making up our stories,
our traditions. Did we bury the Indians? Why, there are
five hundred Indian place names in our State, each with its
legend of war and treason and friendship and love. The
valleys of the Mohawk, the Hudson, the St. Lawrence, and
the Genesee are alive with them as summer fields are alive
with fireflies. Did we drive the Dutch and English back
across the ocean? What nonsense! Look at their ships gliding
on the lakes and fluttering in the bays, while the dour sailors
led by the mighty Captain Kidd seek the hidden treasures.
Ghosts, you sneer, phantoms. Except for this fragile moment
you call the present, what is everything save ghosts and
phantoms?

And here, too, are the "bulbous-bottomed goblins" in
trunk hose and sugarloaf hats, the imps, the gnomes, and
the witches. But the witches were our great-grandparents'
fears and prejudices and hates and superstitions incarnated.
And they tortured the queer old women but all in vain, and

Cotton Mather could not explain the mystery. Maybe he knows better now. Do *we?*

Add to the *folklore* the old familiar songs and ballads, such as "Blue Mountain Song" and "Low Bridge, Everybody Down." Accompanied by dancing, these songs were especially popular in the lumber camps. The canal life was transmuted into appropriate songs, too, the most famous of which is "Fifteen Years on the Erie Canal."

And while we are in this lighter mood, let us take a glimpse at the sports of the Empire State.

The Dutch, as everyone knows, were a great hand at ninepins, and they gave us the bowling alleys; the French gave us their version of billiards; the English introduced cockfighting and animal baiting.

Modern baseball, allegedly invented by Abner Doubleday, started about the middle of the nineteenth century. The first jockey club was organized in 1868, and at about the same time lawn tennis, polo, basketball were introduced. Golf was introduced in Yonkers in 1888. New York City has three big-league baseball clubs, the Yankees drawing the largest share of three million customers each season. Upstate, professional baseball is represented by a number of minor leagues. Boxing and wrestling are almost entirely limited to professional circles, sponsored by local sporting clubs. You will find first class horse-racing at Goshen, Saratoga, Yonkers, and Long Island. In the metropolitan area there are four tracks—Belmont, Jamaica, Aqueduct, and Empire City. Here, too, are five college football teams, drawing one million spectators each season. Boxing, hockey and basketball—the big-time varieties—center at Madison Square Garden. Skiing has recently caught the popular fancy, and thousands of *aficionados* find their way to the ski trails in the Taconics, the Hudson Highlands, the Catskills, the Adirondacks.

And so the Empire State developed from wilderness to magnificence, but while its history has certain individual and unique phases and a world glamour, it nevertheless runs parallel with the history of the entire nation and in many ways illustrates its various stages. There is the gradual change in population from one English stock to an amalgam of many, and from timid colonialism to aggressive independence, from slavish copying of Continental culture to a regional one, to self-confidence in the arts, in letters, in music, in architecture.

As New York became a state the country became a nation, and fortunately so, for in a union of forty-eight states it would not do for one, or a set, to outstrip too much the others or to develop in a totally different manner and become a stranger or strangers, and therefore potential enemies. Only friendly rivalry is the objective of the Empire State, although it contains within its borders more than 10 per cent of the total population of the country, 12 per cent of its wage earners, and produces more than 15 per cent of its manufactured goods. It is the nation's greatest financial, mercantile and cultural center but still a devoted member of the family, and its greater pride is not that it is the Empire State but that it is a State in the United States of America.

20 The Wonders of Man
—Cities

EVEN as the State of New York is rich in Nature's wonders, so is it rich in the wonders its inhabitants have created with brain and muscle and imagination and indomitable will —the cities. And here they are.

ALBANY

Capital of the State. Population 135,000. Inland seaport. You need strong legs and good lung capacity for most of the important businesses are situated on the steep slope of the hill, on which, like a crown, glows the Capitol, surrounded by the State office buildings. The government of the State is similar to that of most other states—bicameral legislature, governor, lieutenant-governor, elected by popular vote.

On September 19, 1609, Henry Hudson anchored the *Half-Moon* in the shallows off the site of the present city. Father Isaac Jogues, the Jesuit martyr, said in 1643 that the settlement was "composed of about 100 persons who reside in some 25 or 30 houses built along the river."

Albany has large factories of felts, textiles, woolens, paper towels. There are ocean-going vessels with cargoes of petroleum, grain, and lumber.

Points of Interest:

The City Hall, French Romanesque style.

The Schuyler Monument, standing on a circular plot in

front of City Hall. Daniel Webster said Schuyler "was second only to Washington in the services performed for his country."

The State Capitol, an imposing, massive granite building. It covers three acres and cost $25 million. *The New York State Education Building*, neoclassic architecture, cost $4 million.

Bleecker Stadium seats 10,000.

Washington Park occupies 90 acres.

If you like to look at statues, look at that of *Robert Burns*, lover of men, deflater of pomposity. The statue is situated east of the *King Fountain* in Washington Park.

The State Executive Mansion, a large red brick building of the Civil War period.

The Schuyler Mansion, museum, built in 1762.

The Port of Albany, one of the largest inland seaports in the United States, cost $13 million (when a dollar was worth a dollar) to complete.

AUBURN

Population, 40,000. Center of shoe manufacturing.

Points of Interest:

The Broome County Courthouse, erected in 1898 of Ohio sandstone, trimmed with bluestone.

Ross Park, more than a hundred acres of wooded slopes and picnic sites.

The Binghamton State Hospital, founded in 1854, a city in itself with power plant, farms, shops, and nurses' homes. It provides for the care and treatment of mental patients.

BINGHAMTON

County seat of Broome County. Population, 81,000. First settlement in 1787. Extensive manufacturing industries, chief of which is the cigar—third in cigar manufacturing in the United States. Many parks—most attractive of which is *Ross Park*, 100 acres.

Points of Interest:

State Armory, Central High School, City Hall, Federal Building, Supreme Court Law Library.

BUFFALO

Population, 600,000, largest industrial and commercial center in upstate New York.

Points of Interest:

The Buffalo City Hall, completed in 1932, 32-story tower dominating 14-story wings flanking the tower.

The New York State Building, neoclassic design.

Soldiers' and Sailors' Monument, erected in 1882.

Grosvenor Library, contains 300,000 volumes.

Mark Twain House, wedding gift of the bride's father. Misfortune after misfortune struck the couple while they were in the house, and two years later they left it and the city.

The Forest Lawn Cemetery with an area of 267 acres, for those who like to meditate upon the transitoriness of all things—and yet draw comfort thereby for their own sorrows.

Delaware Park, 350 acres.

University of Buffalo, campus of 174 acres.

Humboldt Park, popular East Side resort.

Buffalo Harbor, waterfront of 37 miles.

COHOES

City of Albany County. Population 21,000. Formerly part of the Rensselaer Manor. Noted manufacturing center, woolen and cotton mills, collar and shirt factories.

Point of Interest:

Falls 75 feet high, 900 feet wide.

ELMIRA

County seat of Chemung County. First settled in 1788. Population 52,000. Flat valley fringed by wooded hills. Manufacturing center for fire-fighting apparatus, glass bottles, silk goods.

Points of Interest:

Elmira College, one of the earliest colleges for women, founded in 1855.

Woodlawn Cemetery, graves of Mark Twain and his son-in-law, the great pianist, Ossip Gabrilowitsch, whom he resented; both in Langdon plot, eternal neighbors.

Mark Twain Study, on Quarry Farm where American humorist wrote most of his books and also meditated upon, or perhaps even wrote portions of *The Mysterious Stranger* and *What Is Man?*—two of the most pessimistic books in any literature, published posthumously, not to hurt the tender sensibilities of those of his readers who insisted that he must always make them laugh.

ITHACA

County seat of Tompkins County. Has very picturesque scenery, including the Taughannock Falls, 215 feet high, the highest east of the Rocky Mountains. Population 30,000. Though it has an extensive coal trade, its chief economic activity consists in supplying the needs of the 7,000 teachers and students.

Points of Interest:

Cornell University and its campus of 1,500 acres.
City Hall, erected in 1842.

Stewart Park, includes a bathing beach and picnic grounds, and contains a bronze plaque in honor of Louis Agassiz Fuertes, native of Ithaca, famous ornithologist and painter of bird pictures.

KINGSTON

County seat of Ulster County. The Dutch constructed a Fort at the mouth of the Rondout Creek in 1614 and in 1652 a settlement was established. Kingston was the first capital of New York.

Population 30,000. Important trade in coal, cement, lumber and large factories of street railway cars, automobiles and machine-shop products.

Points of Interest:

Soldiers' and Sailors' Monument, Federal Building, The Senate House.

NEW ROCHELLE

Westchester County. First settlement in 1688 by Huguenot refugees from La Rochelle, France. Population 60,000. Primarily a residential suburb of New York and contains many handsome residences and large estates.

Points of Interest:

Hudson Park, City Park, Travers Island with the fine building of *New York Athletic Club.*

Paine Memorial House, ground broken by Thomas A. Edison, ardent admirer of the great author and statesman.

POUGHKEEPSIE

County seat of Dutchess County. First settled by the Dutch in 1698. Population 45,000. Situated midway between New York City and Albany. Manufacturing of blast furnaces, foundries, woodenware, furniture, and hardware specialties. The name in Indian probably means "reed-covered lodge by the little water place." *Multum in parvo*, "Much in little," as the Latin critics used to warn the loquacious orators and poets.

Points of Interest:

U. S. Post Office, FDR laid the cornerstone.

The Smith Brothers Plant, famous for beards and cough drops.

Vassar College, 950 acres of campus.

ROCHESTER

Port of Entry and County seat of Monroe County. Originally the home of the Seneca Indians. First visited by the French who established a French post on Irondequoit Bay in 1710. Population 350,000, third largest city in the State. Plants produce Kodak cameras, optical goods, shoes, clothing, carbon paper.

Points of Interest:

Kodak Tower, 19 stories high, "the nerve center of photography."

Edgerton Park, 62 acres for winter athletics.

Veterans' Memorial Bridge, the longest of the city's, widely praised for its classical architectural beauty.

University of Rochester, started with 60 students in 1850, now has over 6,000 and 600 instructors.

SARATOGA SPRINGS

The word means in Indian "Hillside of the Great River." First settled about 1792. Population 16,000. Leading summer resort with over 50 mineral springs of worldwide reputation for their medicinal properties.

Points of Interest:

The Saratoga Race Track located a mile from city.

Yaddo, an estate of 500 acres and four lakes and landscaped grounds, dedicated to creative artists for the purpose of finding "the Sacred Fire and light their torches at its flame." And Solomon said there was nothing new under the sun. Nothing new? Why, even the Sun must perpetually renew itself or be no more.

SCHENECTADY

County seat of Schenectady County. Originally the site of the chief village of the Mohawk Indians. First settled in 1662 by Arendt Van Corlear. Population over 100,000. The economic life of the city is chiefly dependent upon the plants of the General Electric Company and the American Locomotive Company.

Points of Interest:

The General Electric Plant, 360 buildings on 670 acres.

Schenectady City Hall, outstanding modern building of the city.

Union College, second incorporated college in the State, chartered in 1795.

SYRACUSE

County seat of Onondaga County. The Syracuse region became known through its salt deposits as early as 1653. Ephraim Webster built a trading post in 1786 and was the first settler. Population 210,000. Manufacturing of typewriters, electric appliances, chemicals, soap, perfume.

Points of Interest:

Museum of Fine Arts, exclusively devoted to paintings by American artists.

Burnet Park, 135 acres, including a zoo.

Syracuse University, over 10,000 students.

TROY

County seat of Rensselaer County. Formerly the site which was included in the Rensselaer grant of 1629. Population 75,000. Industrial, educational, and shopping center. Largest shirt-manufacturing plants in the country.

Points of Interest:

Prospect Park, overlooking the River and the Hudson Valley.

Rensselaer Polytechnic Institute, first college of science and civil engineering established in an English-speaking country.

UTICA

County seat of Oneida County. First settled in 1786. Population 100,000. Trading center and largest mill town in Mohawk Valley.

Points of Interest:

Munson-Williams Memorial, home of the Oneida Historical Society.

Utica State Hospital, first State institution for the mentally ill.

WEST POINT

United States Military Reservation, known under the present name since Revolutionary times. It has an area of 3500 acres. Military police at north and south gates supply directory of buildings and information. Visitors are subject to military police regulations.

Two men who did *not* make good at West Point: *Edgar Allan Poe*, kicked out after eight months for insubordination; *James A. McNeill Whistler*, kicked out in his third year for flunking in chemistry. "Had silicon been a gas, I would have been a major general," he said later. But his sketches of cadet life are among the school's prized possessions.

YONKERS

Westchester County adjoining New York City on the North. First settlement in 1650 by Adrian Vander Donck, the first historian of New Netherland, and several Dutch families. Population 150,000. Varied and important industries: sugar refineries, carpet mills, lumber mills, hats, furniture.

Points of Interest:

Philipse Manor House, which from 1872 to 1908 was used as city hall.

Mount St. Vincent Academy, Catholic.

HYDE PARK

A simple tombstone of white marble on which is carved:

FRANKLIN DELANO ROOSEVELT
1882–1945

That is all.

But listen—and you shall hear the voice of the world:

> Sing the glory and greatness
> Of the Chieftain without peer!
> Like Washington victor in war,
> Like Jefferson carver of tablets,

Like Lincoln welder of nations,
Pressing the essence of goodness
From the fruit of pain and of sorrow.

Illumine the Scroll of Story
With the gold of his deeds:
He who banished the fear of fear
And the specter of homeless old age,
He who slew the dragon of hate
Of race against race and faith against faith,
Transmuted the bane of distrust
Into wine of neighbors and friends,
Broke the chains of nations enslaved,
Proclaiming justice for all!

Trumpet in martial notes
His mighty Charter of Freedom,
And the hearts of all men
Shall beat marches of hope and of triumph
At the sound of his name,
And the vision of his image
Shall flame and shall fresco
The altar and dome of their spirits!

Sing the glory and greatness
Of the Chieftain without peer!

21 *The Empire City*

NEW YORK is everything to everyone—the Whore of Babylon, the doomed Nineveh, the Gay Gotham, the City of Freedom, the City of the Heart of Steel, the City of Opportunity, the City of Lost Hopes, the New Athens, Mammon's Lair, the City of Perpetual Motion, the City of Endless Noise, the City of Contrasts, the Carnival of Hell, the Myriad-Ringed Circus, the Orbit of the Earth, Metropolis, Cosmopolis, the Melting Pot, the Paradox, the Sphinx of the New World, the Symbol of Democracy, the Godless City, the City of All Gods, the City of the Towers of Babel, the Capital of the World.

O Lord, grant us labels and spare us thought!

To judge a city by only one of its manifestations is like judging the sea by a jugful of its waters. We miss the waves, the tides, the roar, the gold of the setting sun, the silver of the moon, the boats that cleave its flanks, the treasures that sleep on its bed, the stilled battles which the foams cover as fields of daffodils cover the cemeteries of the Earth.

But first its habitat. It is 226 miles northeast of Washington, 232 miles southwest of Boston, 911 miles east of Chicago. It occupies a little over 300 square miles in the southeastern corner of the Empire State, having a total frontage of 578.4 miles, being 36 miles long at its longest and 16½ miles at its widest.

New York is not one continuous city but rather a miniature United States of its own, composed of five boroughs: Manhattan (22 square miles, the smallest of them all); the Bronx (twice as large); Brooklyn (three and a half times as large); Queens (five times as large); Richmond-Staten Island (twice as large). Each borough is separated from the other by water and could have used it as a frontier, divinely ordained, to be fortified against its neighbors. The ancient cities of Athens and Venice and Genoa and Marseilles were thus conceived and thus dedicated to perpetual warfare. Are we wiser or merely older? Are we wise enough and old enough to understand the larger implications? Are we ready for the New World?

The citizens of our boroughs do have their jealousies and their rivalries, as every good family should have in order to add spice to their quotidian lives. Manhattan is snooty. Brooklyn is belligerent. Bronx has its special "cheer" for both of them. Queens and Richmond are in the process of formulating "attitudes." But they are all united not only by bridges and subways and buses but by cords of loyalty and common interests. They are all good New Yorkers—children of the Empire City of the Empire State.

If you consult your map, you will note that Manhattan has the shape of a stone cleaver ready to strike at Long Island. It begins where the East River branches off into the Sound at Bronx Kills. Adjacent to the north is the only mainland portion of the City—the Bronx. Opposite Manhattan to the west are the Palisades of New Jersey. In the harbor lies Staten Island, southwest of Manhattan.

Had the 1890 generation but known how tough Manhattan is (not its heart, but its bottom), with its thick, unyielding rock, the great architect of the day, Barford Lee Gilbert, would not have said in a *New York Times* interview apropos of the Tower Building, the first skyscraper to be erected:

The mere suggestion of a building 21½ feet wide rising to the height of 160 feet above its footings (13 stories) filled everybody with alarm. The owner was afraid the building would blow over and that he would be subject to heavy fines. . . . One Sunday morning, when the walls of the building were ready for the roof, I awoke to find the wind blow a hurricane. I went down to the skyscraper. A crowd of persons who expected it to blow over stood at a respectful distance to watch the crash. Janitors and watchmen in adjoining buildings and structures across the street moved out. They were afraid of being crushed to death. . . . The building stood as steady as a rock in the sea.

A rock in the sea—that is the true nature of the Manhattan schist—crystalline rock glinting with mica and fated to become the Atlas upholding the mountains of stone and steel which rise from the bay, challenging in grandeur and beauty the masterpieces of Nature.

Gone are the days when a rocky promontory projected from the tip of Manhadoes (Island of the Hills), sheltering Indians who landed in canoes. Over those hills Broadway stretches its glittering body now. Gone, too, are the valleys and the grassy dales where huddled the first settlers, seeking security against their enemies—the elements and beast and man. There were forests and thickets and bushes; there were wolves and foxes and bears and panthers. And even the gentle deer and the strutting turkey could hardly be considered in the nature of friends when they destroyed the crops.

Broadway began to stretch without fanfare and without premonition of its destiny along an Indian trail over hills which were one hundred or more feet above the water. Not all of them have carved within them legends to inspire the young descendants of those early settlers, almost fabulous themselves. On one large knoll rising north of Collect Pond criminals were hanged. In an adjoining hollow Negroes suspected of inciting riots (what an excellent diversion for the whites who complained against their many injustices) were burned alive.

Between the hills were waterholes, or little streams that meandered and got lost, to be found again two centuries later by subway sandhogs, causing them a great deal of trouble. There was Minetta Brook, which wound and wound from the present University Place, dropped into a salt marsh, and thus polluted found its weary terminus in the North River. There was a nameless brook which hummed its way through Tompkins Square into the East River. There was a stream which had a tributary of its own and ran down Beaver Street to be forgotten in the waters of the Hudson.

Drinking water was not obtained by the miracle of turning the spigot. The burghers or their slaves or servants had to go to the public wells in the center of the city and wearily drop and hoist the buckets. Even the pump had yet to make its bow. But there was also the "tea-water-man" who sold the most palatable of the water for a penny bill a gallon.

Not until the overflow from the pump made foul, disease-breeding cesspools did the early citizens build "good pitch pipes, well-hooped with iron" to distribute the water to sub-scribing households. And not until the Revolution was over and the Civil War was fought do we find installed water systems worthy of their names. But no city in all the world has sweeter water now, nor cooler, nor in greater abun-dance than ours.

Manhattan rises gently in the north and reaches its high-est peak on the upper West Side. Another rise culminates with the Cathedral Plateau which drops again at 125th Street, finally to rise at St. Nicholas Heights. Not that you need to be a mountaineer to climb these peaks. Your pulse will quicken a bit and your lungs will have to work a trifle

faster; as for your car, you will have trouble with it only
when the streets are covered with ice and snow. Certainly
you will encounter far greater difficulties entering or leaving
the subway trains during rush hours. Then surely you will
need solid bones, sharp elbows, good feet, and luck, while
brazenness is an excellent lubricant.

The subway is the lodestone of the New Yorker's character. If he has forgotten or discarded on purpose the amenities
once regarded as *sine qua non*—offering seats to ladies, lift-
ing hats, precedence to age—he has shown himself, nonethe-
less, a miracle of patience and good nature. He has accepted
the role of the sardine, adding his own oil of tolerance. He
loves humanity—its heat, its breath, its pressing belly, and its
crushing foot, or else how could he survive?

The ribs of Manhattan are not all of vulgar stone. In the
granite veins of the rocks there are precious stones: garnets,
amethysts, opals, tourmalines, beryls, chrysoberyls—99 species and 170 varieties. But how shall one recognize the truly
precious? Does not the dew transmute fly-dotted spider webs
into bags of pearls? And is not many a pygmy on stilts hailed
as a giant?

But of all the rocks studded or unstudded with jewelry,
the most interesting is the escarpment of the Palisades, which
serves as a carved frame for the Hudson. They are not be-
wilderingly tall, these cliffs, and do not make man seem in-
consequential. They rise about 700 feet, are 350 to 1000 feet
thick, and are of volcanic origin.

Queens is divided into the North and South shores by
northerly hills running the length of Long Island. In Brooklyn large areas of Flatlands, Greenpoint, Williamsburg and
Red Hook have been raised above sea level. The rounded
hills on Staten Island extend in a northeast-southwest chain
about three hundred feet high and are of serpentine rock.

The hills of the Bronx are a part of the foothills and worn extensions of the Green Mountains and the Berkshires.

The Bronx River goes its way in the center of the borough, now seen, now hidden, now barely wetting the stones, now several feet in depth, now cramped into a few in width, now sprawled into three hundred, now a cataract, now an eddy— but generally forgotten and unsung except at Gun Hill Road, where it embraces the statue of a Confederate soldier at whose pedestal it brings its tribute of twigs and fallen leaves and logs and all the nameless things that sail on hopelessly and without destination—vagabonds of the waters.

Who is this soldier, and what is he doing in the path of a running river? Does he symbolize victory, futility, warning —this man with the corroded green overcoat, pancake cap, and carbine kept at ease? The shores of the river have been converted into a park, and old people and young sit on the benches or the grasses or cross the small bridge, always intrigued about the first "Unknown Soldier."

Such is the present face of the Empire City, but in the Great Past the northeastern coast rose a mile higher than now, and Manhattan was not yet an island. Then the Hudson plunged into the maw of a canyon mightier than any man has ever looked upon and trembled.

The last glacier wended its way back to Labrador some 35,000 years ago, leaving the city's contours practically as they are at present. And because the glacier, upon retreating, was only a half-mile thick, the rocks remained practically intact, and therefore, there is but a slim chance for earthquakes. You may sleep in peace in Gotham if your conscience is clear and your stomach does not rock in a sea of liquor.

The giants are gone, but their stunted descendants have not totally vanished, despite the new world of asphalt and stone and hoops of rubber whirling madly in all directions.

There are still a million trees in New York, and there are remnants of woods in squares and parks in Forest Hills, in the Bronx and on Staten Island. And flowers still waft their perfumes from park and garden and many a vacant lot, not to mention the penthouses.

There are more than fifteen thousand acres of City parkland for plant and animal conservation. There are hundreds of species of wild birds, and the geese, the pelicans, and herons are tenderly looked after. And so are the quail and the pheasants. As for the squirrels and the pigeons—they have gnawed and cooed themselves into the hearts of all. The seagulls take care of themselves. The boats drop garbage, and there are young, adventurous fish who stick their heads out of the water to see the world and perish. But maybe it is worth while, even as it used to be worth while to see Naples and die.

Even in Istanbul in the days of the veil and the fez, "man's best friend" was not treated with greater affection and consideration. Whose arm is not dislocated by the powerful pull of the vitamin-fed canine? What fastidious lady has not played nurse to his vagaries? Which sidewalk has not served as his comfort station; to which hydrant has he not added his mite? He brings us pleasure, consolation, humor. And has he not broken down our mid-Victorian attitude toward the lowlier functions of life?

To the City's half-million dogs add a half-million cats. Predestined foes? Let them but know one another when young with brains unprejudiced, let them but share one another's milk bowl and kennel—and where art thou, irrevocable instinct? Go to the beast, Man, and mend thy ways!

There are still fountains here and there with the inscription: "Drink, gentle horses," but the horses no longer pass that way, and the water no longer runs. Even though statistics claim that there are twenty thousand horses in New York, weeks may pass before you will hear their hoofs quadrille nostalgically some early dawn.

As for jackasses, statistics say nothing, but their number is legion, though their ears are trimmed. And rats there are without number. The more innocent ones have tails. Bats are reported in abundance in forsaken lofts and houses, and the ants wait patiently to take over the City and the rest of the earth, if and when mankind commits suicide.

But people must breathe, and the climate of New York, though temperamental, is, generally speaking, moderate and salubrious. The mean temperature is around fifty degrees Fahrenheit. Strangely enough, this coincides with the temperatures of Paris, London, and Berlin.

But what is so rare as a day in October in New York? It is the season of light. The skies are clear; the air is warm. There is sunshine day after day, often without a patch of cloud or an outburst of rain. A riot of hues gently blends into gorgeous designs on the driveways, in the parks and squares, surrounding the towers and steeples and cornices. If good luck is with us this weather may continue into November and the early part of December. For Winter often comes late in this city, but always overstays its welcome. How cold it can get! How the winds can blow! And what slush and what sleet follow the snow!

And then comes Spring, but somehow it cannot extricate itself from the claws of Winter and the pull of Summer, and between the anvil of the one and the hammer of the other, it often dies without having ever lived. And the buds on the trees turn to leaves and there is Summer. All who can, leave the city. But it is as much a habit or a means of showing off one's opulence as a necessity. And many a pater has a cooler and pleasanter summer in town than his family in a box of a hotel in the mountains or by the sea shore.

The poor in the tenement houses, however, have a preview of hell. They do indeed roast and melt, while the rich graciously relinquish to them heaven—*post mortem*.

The harbor is miraculously free of fog—at least as compared to cities similarly situated. The highest heat recorded is 102.3; the coldest spell 14 below zero; the heaviest gale 96 miles an hour.

But New York, at least, has the graciousness of not promising paradisiacal weather which it cannot fulfill. Instead, the wiser of its citizens know that each day, whatever its temperature, is a fragile blossom whose petals curl and drop and whose perfume is forever scattered, and there is no hothouse ingenious enough to keep it from perishing. And so they try to make the best of it. *Carpe diem!*

By the middle of the nineteenth century, New York already had a population of nearly a million. The lower part of the City, which fifty years previously had been largely farmhouses and lots, was crowded with buildings, and the upper part began to develop, while the elevator, without which the City could not grow vertically and defiantly scrape the underbelly of the heavens, was put into operation in 1859.

As soon as man's belly is full, he begins to belly-ache for beauty. The tyrants of old knew this and always mixed circus with flour.

About the middle of the century, then, we see civic organizations demanding space to breathe, and land was bought and Central Park had its birth. And man is a curious animal. He wants to know things—a lot of things—except the naked truth. But he does wish to know facts and he enjoys fancies. And in New York, in the year 1856, the Board of Education took control of the public school system. Oh, what oratorical fuss and vicious machinations to curtail education to the poor! Charity schools, yes. It is much easier to be kind than just. But education as the right of every citizen, that was a different matter altogether. But Justice triumphed. The New Yorkers fought, and fought hard, and therefore they won.

And now, a century later, New York has hundreds of public schools and dozens of high schools and colleges not only for men but also for women. A budget of $500 million is spent yearly upon the schools in Gotham, and nearly forty-one thousand pedagogues dispense knowledge, wisdom, beauty, and at times, unfortunately, prejudice and superstition.

On January 1, 1898, New York became Greater New York —a city composed of five boroughs; and in 1909, when we celebrated the tricentennial of Henry Hudson's arrival on the Island, we were the Great Metropolis of the world. It was the Empire City of the Empire State. It had taller houses than all other cities. It had more telephones, bathtubs, automobiles, electric lights, subways. It had more energy. It had more hope. It had more audacity. It had more ingenuity. Yet something of the village—the hinterland—clung to it. A village without compare in the annals of man, yet still a village. It needed the shock of contact with the world to acquire maturity. The world had come to it for three centuries but it had not gone out to the world.

We need not go in search of misfortune in order to acquire understanding. We have but to wait. In time misfortune opens every door and greets every man. And World War I broke out. And we became conscious of the world. We could no longer be content to have and to hold. What had we, indeed? What could we hold? If the Old World surrendered to tyranny what would become of the New World? We refused to believe that civilized nations would jump at one another's throats. We refused to believe that men would

allow their governments to order them to kill their neighbors, many of whom had been their good friends and good
customers. We refused to believe that *we* would be dragged
into the trenches, into the blood and mud and lice. No, no,
we said, waving our hands like little children in front of our
faces. No, no!

And yet it all happened. Men obeyed their rulers, men
slaughtered their own friends and customers, and we had to
leave our fair shores, and our blood was spilled and was mingled with the blood of foreigners who used to make us laugh
when they arrived in Ellis Island with their bundles on their
backs, or who enraged us when they worked for less money
than we. How much they contributed to our welfare, to our
riches, to our culture, that we did not take the trouble to
learn. That we took for granted. But now here we were—together—on *their* side of the world. Here we no longer
laughed at them. Here we opened our eyes wide and saw
things that bewildered us with their beauty. Here we learned
more charming ways of living, more gracious manners. Indeed, the joke was largely on us.

We lost tens of thousands of men killed and many more
wounded. We spent billions of dollars. We lent other billions
which were never returned. We had inflation and deflation.
We forgot our heroes, and they sold apples on the streets,
and we had our little spree of Prohibition.

New York became the capital of the world, for where the
money is the heart goeth, like a horse who follows the bag of
oats. The New Yorkers never forgot their experiences abroad,
and those who had never crossed the ocean listened, and
their imaginations were fired, and they became part of that
other world, too.

We had our baptism of fire. We survived. But Fate had
even greater things in store for us. Greater and more terrible.

We had grown up. We were no longer villagers. We were townfolk. But that was not enough. We were nationally minded. But that was not enough. The word "international" scared us out of our wits. And so, we went on, whistling in the gathering night. We heard horrible things coming out of the Land-beyond-the-Rhine, but we shrugged our shoulders. None of our business. They murdered the Jews—let them. Purely local matter. Rights of sovereignty. Let the Jew die. We had a society for the prevention of cruelty to animals. We had hospitals. We had foundling homes. We had homes for the aged. We had charitable institutions. We had the Red Cross. We were a kindly people. We were a sensitive people. We were a civilized people. We proclaimed the inalienable rights of all men. But let the Jew die. None of our business. We were a great City—the Empire City. No city had ever had such tall buildings, so much wealth, such power—and yet we shrugged our shoulders, turned our backs, hid our heads in the sands.

And there was justice. . . . And we had World War II!

Now the dead understand—the dead of the villages, the dead of the small towns, the dead of the great cities, the dead of the Empire City—all the dead understand. And all the dead—those who are buried in the waters, and those who are blanching upon the sands, and those whose ashes are tossed by the winds—all call to the living of the Earth: *"You are your brother's keeper!"*

Do we hear them *now?*

22 Melting Pot?

OVER eight million in the Pot and the fire of Americanism under it—continuously fed by one language, the Constitution, the Bill of Rights, history, public schools—"one nation indivisible with liberty and justice for all," soldiers' and sailors' uniforms, miles of white crosses in all parts of the globe, but are we melted? Have we become one?

The young generation so resembles one another that it is difficult to separate them into origins. And yet there never was so much talk of minorities and rights of minorities, races and religions, Jew and Gentile, White and Colored, Nordic and Mediterranean. Shades of the Balkans!

Are flesh and bone less tough than prejudices taught in childhood, than half-truths heard in the home and the street, than ancestral memories?

"On the Island of Manhate and its environs," Father Jogues of the Society of Jesus reported in 1646, "there may well be four or five hundred men of different sects and nations; the Director General told me that there were men of 18 different languages." He did not mention the Indians. The Indian was already a stranger in his own home.

Came the *Dutch*. They gave us some names of streets, the queer topography of the oldest section of the City, delightful legends, and several families whose members have become illustrious in American History. But the Dutch do not form a separate entity now and in that sense have vanished.

The English. While they are part and parcel of the history of the City, they are strangely nonexistent. Those who now speak their language, obey their laws, feed on their literature and tradition, belong to other lands, to other races. The English have immortalized themselves but with little of their own blood. The roots are not biological, yet their blossoms have something of the original perfume, and the fruits the savor.

1848—and the revolutions in Europe and their failure and the vast migration to all parts of the globe. The Earth belonged to man then. The Earth was free. We were not neighbors, but we could become friends and relatives. The trips were long and hazardous, but the gates were open and the arms extended. And millions came to the Land of Freedom, to the Land of Opportunity, to the Golden Land—each according to his hopes and visions. And many a lakh, as the Hindus say—countless thousands—remained in the City and made it the Empire City.

The Germans. In 1664 one-fourth of the Population of New Amsterdam was of German stock. They had come from all parts of the country—Northern Germany, the Rhine district, Hessia, Westphalia, Suabia, and German-speaking Switzerland. A quarter of a century later, a new flood took place, this time from the Palatinate, impoverished by the eternal wars between the French and their neighbors.

Many among them rose to honor and fame and wealth. "Little Germany" conquered the City along the East Side from Houston Street to Yorkville, dotting its northern progress with beer halls, clubs, song and dance and *Gemütlichkeit.*

The Irish. In the year 1683 Sir Thomas Dongan, an Irish Catholic, became governor of the English province of New York. There were a few more hundred of his compatriots in the colony, chiefly blacksmiths, tailors, weavers, and cobblers. But also James Duane, who became New York's first mayor after the Revolution, and thus established a precedent.

But the real migration from Ireland occurred in 1846 and 1847. Famine and hate of the English oppressors drove them in such vast numbers that by the time of the Civil War there were more than two million, many of whom remained in New York City. They had had enough of farming, which for centuries had brought them only poverty and persecution. Now they would become city folk like their English masters, and maybe they, too, would become rich and powerful. What a man hates—and how profoundly—determines his character and his career. The Irish hated poverty and slavery and were determined to get rid of both. They had a tough time of it at first. They were disliked for their nationality and perse-cuted for their religion. But they succeeded at last. Many of them remained poor, but a goodly number achieved wealth and prominence. They added their talents to the City's en-deavors—literary, scientific, industrial—and spiced existence with their sense of humor.

The Italians. In 1524, eighty-five years before Henry Hud-son looked upon that hilly island called Manhattan, Giovanni Verazzano, the Florentine, entered its harbor. The Floren-tines were too deeply involved in their political feuds with other Italian cities of the day to become seriously interested in colonization. And so the Italians discovered the New Con-tinent, gave it its name, and charted some of its rivers and harbors but only established themselves here centuries later, as immigrants, under the stress of poverty.

Even as late as 1880, the Italian population was only twelve thousand. Unlike the Irish who had come from an Anglo-Saxon country and knew the language, and therefore could mingle with everybody, the Italians were forced to cluster

together, many never learning English or the American ways
which seemed to them, as they seem to immigrants from
other parts of the globe, machinelike and heartless.

The oldest settlement was the "Mulberry Bend," which became notorious for its squalor and poverty. The Italians still
live in great numbers in the lower East Side of the City, but
the bulk of the population moved to the Bronx and Brooklyn.

How shall modern man live without streets and railways
and sewers and clothing and houses? So let us do homage
and give our profound thanks to these good people who
have contributed so much to their creation, and who have
so often been maligned and ridiculed. And not only to our
material well being but to our art have the Italians brought
their share. And who having ears shall not bless that nation
which gave us glorious operas and added into the bargain a
Caruso and a Toscanini?

The Jews. About the year 3000 B.C. groups of the Semitic
race began to spread over the Near East. Again and again
they crossed Palestine—the natural bridge between Asia and
Africa. Numberless little sovereign communities sprang up.
A special clan of that race, however, cut itself adrift from
the group and settled on the confines of Canaan. These people
were known as the *Ibrim* (in English, "Hebrews"), from the
Hebrew word *eber*, the "other side."

Crude and unpretentious were their beginnings, but Fate
had in store for them a magnificent and unique history, glorious and tragic beyond compare. They were to develop sages
and saints and prophets and a religion of such vitality that
two other great faiths—Christianity and Mohammedanism—
sprang from it.

The Jewish history is as ancient as the legend of man and
as fresh as an open wound. The ancient part we have in the
catechisms, in the prayers, in the Holy Books. We heard it

as children. We hear it in solemn music and words in all the churches and cathedrals and mosques.

The fresh part took place recently in the concentration camps and the crematoriums of Europe, and is taking place at this moment in Israel.

Twenty-three Jews, refugees from the Inquisition, arrived in New Amsterdam in 1654, and at the close of the eighteenth century the Jewish population in New York numbered only four thousand of Spanish and Portuguese origin. And, although as the historian Lecky says, "Hebraic mortar cemented the foundations of American democracy," referring to the great influence the Old Testament had upon the Puritan Fathers, and their descendants, the Jews themselves were persecuted and all restrictions against voting and holding office were not completely removed until well into the nineteenth century.

It was only in the middle of the nineteenth century that the Jews began coming in great numbers, first from Germany, then from Eastern Europe—Russia, Romania, Austria —in the wake of cruel pogroms. At present the Jewish population of New York is two million. This City would not have been the Empire City without their extraordinary share in business, art, politics, trade, education.

The Irish, the Germans, the Italians and the Jews are the big chunks in the Pot, but there are many middle-sized ones and countless tiny morsels, while some serve only as condiments. All of them, however, are part and parcel of the Empire City, for although there are monuments and parks and museums and buildings requiring the necks of giraffes to behold their uppers, New York is essentially *people*. Other cities in the world surpass it in history, in beauty, in charm, but there is something about the New Yorkers *en masse* that is unique and fascinating.

Their gait is elastic, their eyes and ears are alert, and while they always seem intent upon some tremendously important destination they are invariably ready to stop and listen to any soapbox speaker with flag unfurled advertising futile remedies and pointless merchandise. As for watching *other* people work, that is their most delectable pastime. They are young—that is the explanation in a nutshell, and often the stranger's exasperation.

And how handsome this new generation is—tall, erect, bright-cheeked. Wander about all the boulevards of Paris and Vienna and Madrid, and where shall you see such luscious womanhood? And where, even in the heyday of the world's capitals, were they so well dressed, so many of them? Who shall distinguish here between the millionaire's daughter or wife and the wife and daughter of a worker or a small businessman?

Too bad we have not imitated our Latin neighbors and opened sidewalk cafés, where one could sit and watch the eternal parade. Too bad, for the eye of the male knows no deeper nor more exquisite mystery than the tidal movements of woman's buttocks. From his table, as an astronomer from his observatory, he could watch, measure, and compare.

It can hardly be said, however, that the manners or the speech of the inhabitants of the Empire City equal their appearance. Language, man's greatest glory, is often mutilated. What is this rasping, nasal, unaccented thing—a human voice, which should be more soothing than the running brook, more pleasant than the song of bird? And this curt reply, this impatient gesture, this supercilious grimace—are they manifestations of the human soul? Are we becoming

peacocks—magnificent plumage and horrible sounds? Shall
we imitate the ways of the ourang and the bear?

But let us stir the smaller particles in the Pot, and present
them:

HARLEM

155th Street on the north, 110th Street on the south, the
Harlem and East Rivers on the east and Amsterdam Avenue
on the west—a ghetto of nearly a half million people with
skins from delicate nut-brown to ebony, and not a few red-
heads and blonds. Whose blood flows through their veins in
greater quantity, that of the white man or of their African
ancestors?

Not all the gold hoarded in Fort Knox would be sufficient
to pay the wages owed to the generations of the Negro
slaves since the first eleven were brought to New Amsterdam
in 1626.

The Negro is no longer sold at the auction block, nor is the
soul-corroding indignity of segregation in cars and trains and
schools heaped upon him in New York. But these are nega-
tive things. The Negro wants to know why he cannot live in
any part of the City that he desires and can afford; he wants
to know what to do with a college degree if the professions
are closed to him; he wants to know why a man's skin, not
his character, not his abilities, should matter in a nation conceived in liberty and dedicated to justice for all. Not all the
pompous patter of all the pious pundits can explain away the
awful wrong.

Meanwhile, the Negroes in Harlem live in squalor, cramped
in houses unfit for human habitation. And yet where else can
you hear such Gargantuan laughter; where else see such
abandon to life and gaiety? And where else such awakening
to art, science, literature? Every day new names are added

to the scroll of achievement, despite restrictions and heart-rending discriminations.

The Negro is supposed to embody the romance of American life, but this romance is overlaid with shadows of tragic premonitions. Civilization is gauged not by the jubilation of the majority but by the laments of the minority. Civilization is the elimination of scapegoats.

THE BALKANS—AND THEIR NEIGHBORS

The Greeks. We are warned to beware of the gifts of the Greeks, and yet what people in all history have given us more magnificent gifts than the ancient Hellenes? Or is it for that very reason that the saying originated? We fear the gifts of enlightenment. Ignorance is so sweet a sleep.

The Greeks in our City have added, for our comfort and pleasure, restaurants and night clubs; for romance, flower shops. And so these 30,000 people from the land where democracy was born in Europe, fill our stomachs and thrill our hearts. That is "well done" for any one.

The Yugoslavs, Serbs, Croats, Slovenes. Ten thousand in all, largely dwelling around 23rd Street and 10th Avenue. How often had these people been at one another's throats at home, and yet, here, who has ever heard of revolutions among them, or wholesale murders? Is it merely good manners in public, or the flame of Americanism under the Pot which has melted away some of the sharp corners of their contentions?

Tiny as this community is, it has contributed to art and music and industry, and science has become much richer by the work of Nicola Tesla and Michael Pupin.

The Hungarians. The Magyars in this City number about fifty thousand. They love music, the dance, the theater, and recently they have proved themselves lovers of freedom and fighters against tyranny.

The Czechoslovaks. The Czechs and Slovaks, forty thousand strong in this City, are industrious and respected citizens, who have contributed to our arts and crafts.

The Russians. Only about 2 per cent (and mostly Ukrainians) of those registered as Russians are of the Orthodox faith. The rest are Jews. The first wave of immigration began about 1880, mostly peasants. After the Revolution, the "White Russians" took refuge here to the tune of about five thousand.

SCANDINAVIANS

Nordics though they be, the *Scandinavians* of New York somehow kept their identity intact and, unlike the Dutch and the English, have not become a mere influence but have remained a physical reality. Indeed, they have not even merged among themselves, and so the *Danes,* the *Norwegians,* and the *Swedes* have retained their individual native cultures and modes of life.

The majority of these people came over during the great European migration in the middle of the nineteenth century, the years of man's wild hopes. Most of the immigrants settled in the vast farming regions of the Middle West and followed the traditional agricultural life of their ancestors. Out of the half-million Danes only twenty thousand remained in New York; out of the million Norwegians only sixty thousand; out of one and a half million Swedes, only seventy thousand.

The greater number of the Scandinavians who remained in the City became mechanics, seamen, and skilled workers in the building trades. Politically conscious, the majority are members of various unions. Many among the leaders of unionization were Swedes, who had learned something about the value of unions during the Swedish general strike in 1909.

These are quiet and unobtrusive people, and New York is not much aware of their presence, except when they have a hankering for *smorgasbord*—the interminable *hors-d'oeuvres* —and go in search of Swedish restaurants.

SPANISH-SPEAKING PEOPLE

Three-quarters of a million residents of our City have Spanish as their mother tongue. They are not Spaniards from Spain, since those who had to leave Spain preferred South America. These represent, on the contrary, a rich variety of social and racial backgrounds.

There are the *Puerto Ricans,* for instance, who are American citizens, although this does not help them much since the vast majority are considered colored and must suffer accordingly. Then there are the *Cubans,* many of whom are exiles awaiting the overthrow of their government in order to return and be followed as exiles by those now in power. Those who come from *Argentina, Chile,* and *Uruguay* are usually Latin with some Indian mixture. *Mexicans* are generally mestizos, white and Indian. The few *Peruvians, Ecuadorians,* and *Dominicans* have Indian and mulatto blood.

Generally speaking, the standard of living of these people is low, most of them being unskilled laborers and domestics. Still, they are a jolly lot, when they do not sink in monumental melancholy, and they provide much of the music and the dancing in the cabarets both in Harlem and in other parts of the City.

THE NEAR EAST

Syrians and *Armenians* who had the good fortune to escape the Turkish *yataghans* reached New York toward the end of

the nineteenth century. Not many of them, for not many
escaped. Altogether, the Syrians number thirty thousand and
the Armenians twenty thousand. Some Turks, too—three hundred of them managed to decamp, for His Majesty, the Sick
Man of Europe, would not allow his nationals to leave the
Empire. He needed butchers to slaughter and sheep to fleece.

The Syrians are mainly importers, dealing in embroideries,
laces, linens, brassware. The Armenians engage in the whole
range of the City's occupation. The Turks are generally unskilled laborers.

THE ORIENT

Before the Second World War the *Japanese*, headed by
the powerful House of Mitsui of Tokyo, who occupied a
whole floor in the Empire State Building, were engaged
mainly in large-scale importing. At any rate, the two thousand Japanese in New York were reasonably prosperous.
Why didn't those who supported the Emperor's War in 1941
listen to Hasebe Otoshi, their good poet, who lived around
700 A.D.? He wrote of discomforts of war and of soldiering.

> On this frosty night when clash
> The bamboo leaves in the wind,
> Better than these nine coats I wear
> My lady's limbs would warm me.

The Chinese. The proverb, "A Chinaman's chance," indi-
cates how precarious his life was in America. He was not a
slave yet he worked for almost nothing, was insulted and
ridiculed, and could never aspire to citizenship. American
scholars and historians wrote about the great and ancient
civilization which was China, and men of letters translated
the outstanding verse of the poets of the various dynasties,
but to the New Yorker a Chinaman was a laundryman or a

domestic worker, yellow and therefore eternally inferior, while Chinatown was a den of opium and iniquity. And there were the "tongs," the Chinese secret organizations, and the terrible feuds, the gambling, and the murders.

We have omitted continents, nations, principalities, colonies, races, colors, for it was not our purpose to present a total photograph of the inhabitants of the Empire City but rather something of an impressionistic painting—a dot here, a dab there, a line, a curve. Certainly we did not mean to be neglectful of anyone not herein mentioned. On the contrary, let it be known that humans in every part of the globe, every cranny and crevice, have their representatives in this City, and that each contributes to its glory, its joys, its sorrows, its inadequacies, its follies, even though it be no more than by the shadow of a tint, the soupçon of an aroma, the sigh of an echo, the dream of a dream. And so, to all and sundry, salute!

CHOW

By now you are probably hungry. Of course, you may drop in to any of the hundreds of automats and cafeterias or the thousands of nondescript restaurants along the avenues, in the side streets, everywhere. There is always chow to be gotten in New York from sunrise to sunrise. More than fifty million pounds of foodstuffs pour into the City every twenty-four hours, and yet at no time is there more than a three-day supply of perishable foods on hand.

But you, no doubt, have an adventurous stomach. Well, then, the world entire is at your command. Every type of morsel that man puts into his mouth, cooked or baked or roasted, every spice, every sauce, every juice, every concoction nameless or named beyond the possibility of your utterance, you can obtain. Aladdin's lamp could not evoke tables more fantastic, more sumptuous, more delicate, more indigestible, and hardly more swiftly.

Let's start with *Chinatown.* You can find Chinese restaurants strewn throughout the City, but Chinatown guarantees that it will serve you dishes that could have graced the tables of the mandarins of old, even that most magnificent of them all, at which the Melancholy Emperor used to nibble from golden bowls, sighing: "More gorgeous still are the banquets hungry beggars dream of."

Traveling due north and east by bus or subway or taxi or preferably by foot, that best of all vehicles, you will reach *Second Avenue* where your stomach will be regaled (or ruined) by *Russian, Jewish, Romanian, Hungarian* dishes in more or less their habitat.

Farther up, and more westward between 21st and 32nd Streets, you will find *Armenian, Syrian, Turkish* eating places. As you drink their coffee, strong and sweet and delicately scented with the perfume of roses, you will dream of harems and seven-veiled dancers—all seven veils less weighty than the wings of butterflies and more diaphanous than the limpid waters which fall into the golden fountains gracing the Pasha's gardens.

Farther up still, towards Broadway and the Avenue of the Americas, you will come across *Italian, Hindu, Mexican, Spanish* and *French* cuisines. The French, naturally, will claim your priority. What nation ever so profoundly understood how close the stomach is to the soul, and that by delighting the one you uplift the other? If the floor is strewn with sawdust, the walls are smudged with soot, and the waiters are dressed as apaches, do not be frightened. It's only a polite (but not innocent) imitation of the bistro of the dark alleys of Paris. You will not be murdered, only you will pay double the usual prices—and is that robbery? The food, however, will be excellent there even as it is in the clean French places.

If you yearn for the super-exotic that people speak in whispers only, you will have to inquire about them—in whispers. As for night clubs which are not a bit clubby, and cabarets where couples dance like embattled Indians or press breast to breast like giant pigeons whose wings are vaguely ruffled by the wind, hail a taxi. The chauffeur will take you there.

VAGABONDING

You will surely wish to see the sights which New Yorkers promise themselves to see, but postpone and postpone until some relative from out of town drags them along.

The Battery, a small park about twenty acres at the southern end of Manhattan, where the ninety-two guns were mounted in 1693 as defense against the French who were desirous to take the Island of Many Hills for the glory of *Le Roi Soleil.*

A little farther off, where the *Custom House* now is, there was a rocky ledge which the Dutch called *Schreyers' (Weepers') Hook.* From here the homesick would watch the boats leave for the motherland.

At the Southern tip of Battery Park, you will find the ferry which takes you to the *Statue of Liberty*, gift of the people of France to the people of the United States. Inside the pedestal there is a bronze tablet on which you will read the poem by Emma Lazarus, Jewish poetess, who died in 1889:

> Give me your tired, your poor,
> Your huddled masses yearning to breathe free . . .
> I lift my lamp beside the golden door.

Read and ponder—what availeth bigness if greatness is dead? Near *Number 1 Broadway* you will see a small oval park called *Bowling Green,* where the Indians sold Manhattan to Peter Minuit. Stroll on a while, and when you come to *Broad Street,* look for *Fraunces' Tavern,* housed in one of the oldest buildings of the City. Go on farther until you come to *Wall Street,* where few break banks and millions break necks. At the head of Wall Street you will see *Trinity Church,* one of the wealthiest parishes in the world. Walk about the cemetery behind it. Alexander Hamilton and Robert Fulton are buried there. Read some of the inscriptions on the tombstones and their excellent advice to the passers-by full of vanity and gall. For who shall know the true value of something if not he who has lost it?

You may come across the one with no name or dates, but the following poem:

> The things I wished to do
> I left undone,
> I spent my sweat and blood
> On things I hated most.
> Daily, on Life's anvil stretched
> Her hammer twisted me,
> Until the man I yearned to be
> Had vanished in the blows,
> And I was forced to live
> A hated stranger.
>
> . . . .
>
> O gentle passer-by
> Who lieth here,
> Myself
> Or he I would not be?

If further interested, you may visit *St. Paul's Churchyard* on Broadway between Vesey and Fulton Streets, where you may read the following:

How loved, how valued once,
It avails thee not,
To whom related
Or by whom begot
A heap of dust alone
Remains of thee
'Tis all thou art
And all the proud shall be.

Continue on Broadway and you will reach *City Hall* and its park. Like a dwarf of a father who has sired giants, City Hall is flanked by colossal buildings, more or less subsidiary to itself—*Municipal Building, Federal Building, Criminal Courts Building,* etc.

Follow east of the park and you will reach *Brooklyn Bridge.* When it was completed in 1883, the event was celebrated as a national holiday. It was "the eighth wonder of the world." Then there was drama attached to it, as there is to all "wonders." The engineer, John A. Roebling, spent the twelve years required to construct it in bed partially paralyzed, due to an accident. His wife, who acted as his intermediary throughout the tragic years, was the first woman to cross the bridge.

Meanwhile you will have seen a portion of the *Bowery.* During the Dutch regime the *bouweries* were the chief farm district, and the finest part of them, which contained orchards and was known as the Great Bouwerie, belonged to no less a personage than Mynheer, the Governor Petrus Stuyvesant, who knew how to feather his nest without dirtying it too much.

By 1673 the Bouwerie Lane had become a promenade for "ladies and gentlemen." Later still, the Bowery was the main artery for travel in and out of the City.

Today the Bowery has lost not only its original glamor but

also the glamor of the tramp and the rebel against work and society which it had during the latter part of the nineteenth century and the first decade of the twentieth, making the fortune of more than one novelist and short-story writer. Now it is drab and dismal, and the lurid posters in front of its moving picture houses only emphasize its misery like an old man's lascivious laughter.

Bounded by Fifth Avenue on the east, Christopher Street on the south, the North River on the west, and 14th Street on the north, is *Greenwich Village*. Get lost among its crazy, meandering streets, with incredible angles and curves, with quaint little houses, some a century old, with dilapidated tenements, with little garden plots, with ancient vine-covered walls, with restaurants with preposterous signs—wander about and shed a tear for all the dead dreams and the visions and the hopes, mighty Goliaths, brave and defiant, struck by the stones of the puny Davids of Reality.

The Village had a worthy history before it became a legend and a scandal. Next to the Battery it was the oldest settlement, and many of the élite of the first two centuries lived there. And there lived, too, the Great Commoner of Mankind, Thomas Paine—lived the last painful years of his magnificent and tragic life. And there he died.

You may still locate the house, if you care to look for it. There is nothing picturesque about it—no patina of antiquity—nothing charming or lovely. Rather, a poor old, wooden thing with ugly, dingy rooms. What matters it? What matters what the evil tongues wagged, what the evil hearts pulsed? As for Tom Paine, "the sun needs no inscription to distinguish it from darkness."

And while around the Village, look at the Arch on *Washington Square*. It was designed by Stanford White to commemorate the centenary of George Washington's inauguration.

Now if you will continue your itinerary you will reach 34th Street and be confronted with the tallest house in the world —*The Empire State Building*—102 stories above ground and crowned by beacons whose rays, miles long, pierce fog and cloud, proclaiming to all the world its stature without compare. Go up. Stop at the 86th floor where there is a wide esplanade with lounge and restaurant. Then continue rising as far as they will take you, and look about. See the rivers, the boats, the hills, the parks, the roofs of houses, the marvelous sunset—everything—but do not look down at the people. They'll appear so tiny and insignificant, and ridiculous, and you'll seem so terribly important. You'll forget your true size, for you'll include in the measurement of yourself the building that upholds you. Man must look at man level to level—face to face—eye to eye. That is the meaning of democracy. The rest is commentary.

Some blocks farther up you will come face to face with two lions sitting comfortably on their haunches even as the building sits over which they keep vigil. Why lions in front of the *New York Public Library?* To remind you that the pursuit of knowledge is not the business of timid mice but requires courage, boldness, power—attributes of the only king who has any validity.

Enter and you will find refreshing the peace and calm of the place after the turbulence of the streets. Besides, the million books in all languages, there are fine paintings, exquisite bindings, beautiful frescoes, and in the music room you may listen to records you have been wishing to hear but were unable to obtain.

Out again, continue, and you will reach *Rockefeller Center*. It is a great complex—the symbol of New York's power, adolescence, restlessness and, at night, when the Center takes on a certain softness, the essential kindliness, the sentimentality of its inhabitants. It is not an achievement of great architecture, but rather an effort. Everywhere one senses that the architects had problems beyond their capacities, not because they were not first-class men, but because what is appropriate architecture for this immense metropolis, what expresses it most adequately, has not yet been resolved. It is all flux, movement, growth.

At 59th Street *Central Park* opens. Opposite the Plaza is the statue of *General Sherman* on horseback, by Saint-Gaudens, considered one of the finest monuments in New York. The park continues up to 110th Street, between 5th and 8th Avenues—two and a half miles long, a half-mile wide, nine miles of driveways, six miles of bridlepaths and thirty miles of walk. There are lakes with ducks and geese and rowboats to hire. Sailors on leave are invariably manning them, giving the ludicrous appearance of bronco-busters breaking in children's rocking horses. There are streams and charming bridges and kiosks and music and dancing malls, and a fair-sized zoo, and on 82nd Street the *Metropolitan Museum of Art*. Is a museum a glorified mausoleum as some claim, or a vast treasure house perpetually alive? Temperament, professional interest, training, all enter into the judgment. Not to mention the incontrovertible fact that those who bark at another's fame have none of their own to trumpet.

In three-quarters of a century the Metropolitan has become one of the best stocked museums, and is destined, perhaps, to outstrip them all if the tendency continues for American collectors to bequeath their treasures either upon their death or when they weary of toying. All art has its roots in the people and sooner or later must go back to the people. What availeth greed? There is no hierarchy of the dead.

But while at 59th Street, go some blocks west and you will come to *Columbus Circle*. There, atop a tall, ornate pillar, stands the Grand Admiral, the planet in his hand. Does he measure its immensity or the niggardliness of its heart? Does he remember the moment of glory which was his or the days of misery and disgrace which ended his career? Is this the world he would have wished to discover? He went in search of gold for the king; would he have accepted freedom for the people?

Facing Christopher Columbus is the *Coliseum*, a vast building dedicated entirely to the business of putting on fairs —trade gatherings, expositions, displays of all things that men and women wear, sit on, ride in, use for kitchen and bedroom and office, use for water and air and surface of the earth. And, naturally, since the Coliseum is in New York, which has no rival, so it, too, has no rival. Unique! And since we still have the ways of the *nouveau riche*, we shall not fail to tell you that it cost $35 million to build. Whether it will please you as a piece of architecture will depend upon your taste. Do you like the modern coldness, severity, angularity, or do you hanker for grace, curve, ornament?

At 77th Street and Central Park West you will find the *Museum of Natural History*—filled with wonders gathered from all the corners of the Earth, even including meteors from heaven, black stones for worshippers of some new religion. The tiniest bug visible to the naked eye and stuffed monstrous dinosaurs and mastodons which occupy entire halls vie with one another for your attention.

In connection with the museum, visit the *Hayden Planetarium*—the theater of the skies, the universe in a nutshell, its true size, perhaps, save for our illusion.

There are other museums, if you are museum-minded— *The Museum of Modern Art*, 11 West 53rd Street; the *Bache*

Collection, 814 5th Avenue; the *Frick Collection,* 1 East 70th
Street; *The New York Historical Society,* 170 Central Park
West (a treasure house for the lover of history and the student researching); *The Whitney Museum of American Art,*
10 West 8th Street; *The Museum of the City of New York,*
104th Street and 5th Avenue (ship models, toys, costumes
from the beginning of the City's history).

Now go westward to *Riverside Drive.* You can walk along
the shore for a few miles and have the impression that you
are on the deck of a steamer. Sometimes the Hudson is as
smooth and shiny as a window pane that's spotted here and
there and cracked at the corners. The River is not at its best
then. On windy days, however, there are veritable waves,
ermine-crested, and the air is scented with the salt of the sea.
Then you know you are dealing with a river that has seen
much history and belongs to the aristocrats of waters. Now,
if you wish, you may stop to pay your respects to *Grant's
Tomb* at 122nd Street, more out of patriotism than admiration for his resting place, a weak imitation of Napoleon's
Tomb in Paris. Across the street, you may wish to look at the
statuettes carved on the doors and on the sides of the *Riverside Church.* One of them is that of Professor Albert Ein-
stein. A definite departure in Christian Church technique.
You may also wish to enter. It is open the greater part of the
day.

Now you may take the bus on the Drive and go to *The
Cloisters,* situated in *Tryon Park* at 190th Street. Fort Tryon
Park, fifty-six acres, is the highest ground in Manhattan and
a worthy vis-à-vis for the Palisades, here no longer infested
with obnoxious advertisements. During the Revolution the
Fort was a focal point, and there are many romantic tales
connected with it. The famous American sculptor, George
Grey Barnard, while in France tenderly collected the pillars

and other pieces of abbeys which serve as the chief parts of the *Cloisters*. There are, besides, a collection of fifty medieval sculptures and primitive paintings, not to mention the truly exquisite "unicorn" tapestries, equalled only, at the proper season, by the color scheme and design of the flowerbeds surrounding the *Cloisters*.

Now to the *Bronx*. See *Fordham University*. See *Bronx Park*—seven hundred acres—and its magnificent *Zoo*, probably the finest in the world, including the one in Hamburg. See, if you have a penchant for poetry, *Poe's Cottage*, Kingsbridge Road and the Grand Concourse. Here Poe lived (so to say) during the last three years of his unhappy career in time and space. Here he wrote many of his poems, including "Annabel Lee," "Ulalume," and "Eureka." Here Virginia, his beloved child wife, died of cold and starvation. In the small park surrounding the cottage there used to be a metal bust of Poe. Youngsters carved the usual invocations to Eros. And some, more enterprising, carried it off and sold it for junk. It was melted. The stone pedestal lingered on a while, then it, too, vanished. All ye seekers after immortality, ponder on it! And while you are pondering, go to the *Hall of Fame, New York University*, University Heights.

Now *Brooklyn*, borough of parks and cemeteries and historic houses, and a great future, and *Coney Island*, the most astounding, the most colossal, the most renowned, the greatest show on earth—accommodates one million daily!

As for *Queens* and *Richmond*—mainly residences and churches and potentialities.

New York is the Center of the Earth, for here are forgathered representatives of almost every nation. Some call it a debating society, some the salvation of man, some would destroy it, some would give it power beyond the sovereignty of the individual countries—the *United Nations!*

And so, when you have finished your visits of the City, you will do well to visit that building which harbors all the cities. You will travel (without travel's infinite inconveniences) to all the corners of the world.

The building may disappoint you as architecture, the speeches of the delegates may bore you, the exhibits may seem flat and colorless, but when you are back at your desk or in your kitchen you will feel now and then the thrilling awareness that for some minutes you were not only American but Man. And you will hope that perhaps you have witnessed the thread that will lead mankind out of the maze and into the light of peace.

23 *Hail and Farewell*

BY common consent every man is entitled to a bit of folly, roguery, prejudice, falsehood, baseness, treachery, superstition—ingredients essential for his survival. As with the individual, so with masses of men—as with states, so with the Empire State.

Therefore you will feel at home when you visit us, and you *should* visit us. And you will find that despite many shortcomings, the Empire State is a good state and a great one and a hospitable one.

It will help much if you bring with you tolerance and good will and enthusiasm and a sense of humor—which is a sense of proportion. And needless to remind you—some money.

Be our honored guest; the guest for whom the gate is swung wide open and the arms are stretched joyfully forth; the guest who brings gracious greetings from many friends; the guest whose visit is a cup which refreshes—full, but not too deep, that the taste may not pall and the sparkle may not be buried in the dregs—the guest whom the host accompanies far into the road, reluctant to let depart, coaxing another visit in the near future.

A Selected Bibliography

BACON, EDGAR MAYHEW. *Hudson River from Ocean to Source.*

CARMER, CARL L. *The Hudson.*

CHAPIN, ANNA ALICE. *Greenwich Village.*

FEDERAL WRITERS' PROJECT. *New York Panorama.*

MACATAMNEY, HUGH. *Cradle Days of New York.*

MANHATTAN COMPANY, THE. *"Mannahatin," The Story of New York.*

NUTTING, WALLACE. *New York Beautiful.*

PARKER, ARTHUR C. *The Archeological History of New York.*

PETERSON, EVERETT. *Landmarks of New York.*

SHEPHERD, WM. R. *The Story of New Amsterdam.*

STRUNSKY, SIMEON. *No Mean City.*

THOMPSON, H. W. *Body, Boots and Britches.*

ULMANN and STRACHAN. *Tales of Old New York.*

WILSON, RUFUS ROCKWELL. *New York Old and New.*

WORDEN, HELEN. *Here Is New York.*

Index